Emergence

HOW MODERN CONVENIENCE IS DUMBING DOWN OUR CHILDREN AND WHAT PARENTS AND SCHOOLS CAN DO ABOUT IT

Jonathan P. Strecker, EdD

Prometheus Books

Essex, Connecticut

Ⓟ Prometheus Books

An imprint of Globe Pequot, the trade division of
The Globe Pequot Publishing Group, Inc.
64 South Main St.
Essex, CT 06426
www.globepequot.com

Copyright © 2026 by Jonathan Strecker

All rights reserved. No part of this book may be reproduced in any form or by any electronic or mechanical means, including information storage and retrieval systems, without written permission from the publisher, except by a reviewer who may quote passages in a review.

British Library Cataloguing in Publication Information Available

Library of Congress Cataloging-in-Publication Data available
ISBN 9781493094257 (paperback) | ISBN 9781493094264 (epub)

CONTENTS

List of Figures	ix
Preface: Coddiwomple	xi
Introduction	1

PART I: THE FOUNDATIONS OF EMERGENCE — 3

1 The Tricolon: The Magic of Three	5
Emergence	7
Complex Solutions to Complex Problems	12
2 A Bleak Future: Surviving an Era of Intrusive Convenience	13
A Child's Wish	13
Fractal Learning	16
Relationship Between Convenience and Self-Development	17
Intellectual Decline	19
Intelligence Quotient Increases—Flynn Effect	20
Intellectual Declines	21
Social Engagement Decline	21
Social/Emotional/Physical Declines	22
Trust Declines	22
What Else Is Contributing to Our Decline?	25
Reason for Educational Decline	26
News Media	28
Social Media	30
The Importance of Mindset	30
Summary	33
3 Thriving in Complexity: Grappling with Order and Chaos	35
Elliot: An Example of Simplistic Advice	36
How to Think About Complexity	39

Active Complexity	40
The Box System: Striking a Balance Between Order and Chaos	42
Summary	44

4 Privileges and Disadvantages: Helping Children Understand and Overcome Their Initial Conditions — 45

Maslow's Hierarchy of Needs: A Framework for Reflection	49
Physiological Needs	50
Safety Needs	50
Love and Belonging	52
Esteem Needs	54
Self-Actualization	57
Summary	58

PART II: ACHIEVING EMERGENCE: THE FIVE INTELLIGENCES — 59

5 Developing Physical Intelligence — 61

A Wake-Up Call	62
A Crisis in Health	63
The Physical Health Damage Done by Educational Decision-Making, Media Manipulation, and Virtual Existence	65
Educational Reform	65
Sensationalized News Media	66
Virtual Existence	66
The Brain-Body Connection: Protecting Cognitive Function and Well-Being	67
Impacts	68
Small Steps Toward a Positive Tipping Point	69
The Power of the Extra Degree	72
Applying Bloom's Taxonomy to Physical Development	72
Remember	73
Understand	73
Apply	75
Exercise: Energize Your Body and Mind	76
Nutrition: Fuel Your Body, Nourish Your Soul	77
Sleep: Recharge and Renew	78
Analyze	78
Exercise	78

Nutrition	79
Sleep	80
Evaluate	81
Create	81
Summary	82
6 Intellectual Development	**83**
It's Never Too Late to Change Our Path	83
A History of Our Intellect: Rise and Fall	85
The Damage Done by Modern Technology	87
Applying Bloom's Taxonomy to Intellectual Development	90
Remember	90
Understand	92
Apply	97
Analyze	99
Evaluate	102
Create	103
Summary	104
7 Social Development	**105**
Love on the Spectrum	105
The Social Damage Done by Modern Technology	107
What Does Community Look Like?	109
Applying Bloom's Taxonomy to Social Development	110
Remember	110
Understand	111
Introversion	111
Extroversion	111
Apply	114
Social Awareness	115
Social Facility	118
Analyze	121
Evaluate	123
Social Awareness	124
Social Facility	124
Create	124
Summary	125

8 Emotional Development — 127
- Chicago Road Rage — 127
- Emotions—A Primal Force — 128
- The Emotional Damage Done by Modern Technology — 131
- Applying Bloom's Taxonomy to Emotional Development — 132
- Remember — 132
- Understand — 133
- Apply — 137
- Analyze — 140
- Evaluate — 141
- Create — 142
- Summary — 143

9 Ethical Development — 145
- Jury Duty: An Ethical Roller Coaster — 145
- The Weight of Ethical Decisions — 147
- Two Perspectives on Ethics — 150
- Immanuel Kant — 151
- Bruce Weinstein — 153
- The Damage Done by Modern Technology — 155
- Ethics in Society — 157
- Applying Bloom's Taxonomy to Ethical Development — 158
- Remember — 158
- Understand — 159
- Apply — 161
- Analyze — 162
  - Ethical Considerations — 162
- Evaluate — 164
- Create — 164
- Summary — 165

10 Complexity of Development: The Interrelation of the Five Intelligences — 167
- Emergence: A Path to Transcendence — 168
- Combining Your Attributes: An Unstoppable Superpower — 169
- Mastering Social and Emotional Intelligence — 171
- Mastering Physical and Intellectual Intelligence — 171

Mastering Physical, Social, and Ethical Intelligence	172
Mastering Intellectual, Social, Emotional, and Physical Intelligence: Incompetent Ethical Development	173
Mastering Intellectual, Social, Emotional, and Ethical Intelligence: Incompetent Physical Development	174
A Holistic Approach to Development	175
Transcendent Emergence: Mastering the Five Intelligences	177
Summary	179

PART III: ACHIEVING EMERGENCE: THE FIVE INTELLIGENCES — 181

11 Bringing Emergence to Fruition — 183
    Be Sure of Your Vision — 186
    Passion: The Driving Force — 187
    Expertise: Mastering the Learning Process — 189
    Goals: The Roadmap — 195
    Positive Mindset: The Fuel — 198
    Discipline: The Guardrails — 200
    Resilience: The Armor — 202

Acknowledgments — 205
Notes — 207
Bibliography — 213

FIGURES

1.1	Sierpinski Triangle	8
1.2	Amorphous Sierpinski Triangle	9
1.3	Five Intelligences	11
2.1	Amorphous Sierpinski Triangle	15
2.2	Sierpinski Triangle	16
2.3	Collapsing Structure	17
2.4	Relationship Between Convenience and Self-Development	18
2.5	Relationship Between Convenience and Self-Development TP	19
2.6	Flynn Effect	20
2.7	IQ Trends—Norwegian Recruits	20
2.8	Declines in Social Engagement	21
2.9	Declines in Sleep, Social Interaction, and Happiness	22
2.10	Trust Declines	23
3.1	Edge of Chaos	41
3.2	Box System	43
4.1	The Inequitable Climb	48
4.2	Maslow's Hierarchy	49
5.1	Tommy Mygrant	71
5.2	Bloom's Taxonomy (Revised 2001)	73
5.3	Triad of Health	76
6.1	Brain	99

7.1	Social Madness	108
7.2	Rotary Club's Four-Way Test	113
7.3	The Four Components of Social Awareness	118
8.1	Emotional Contagion	129
8.2	Emotions Wheel	136
8.3	Unconscious Incompetence to Unconscious Competence	138
9.1	Moral Dilemmas	149
9.2	Immanuel Kant	151
9.3	Trolley Problem	161
10.1	Complexity	170
10.2	How the Five Attributes Overlap and Reinforce One Another	176
11.1	From the Perspective of a Child	183
11.2	Bloom's Taxonomy (Revised 2001)	189
11.3	SMART Goals	196
11.4	Vision Sequence	203

PREFACE

Coddiwomple

Before accepting advice, it is important to understand the life experiences of the person offering it. My own journey, like many of yours, has been filled with challenges and struggles—the type of adversity that might break a person. And yes, there were dark days. However, now that I have experienced a life well lived, I've found that intellectual hardship, social isolation, emotional fatigue, ethical challenges, and physical turmoil are the very tools we can wield to sculpt us into the best versions of ourselves. Let me begin with a single word that represents the beginning of my journey.

"Coddiwomple" is such an amusing word. As far as I know, it hasn't been included in any formal dictionaries, but I believe it describes my early educational experience perfectly. The term Coddiwomple is slang that describes a journey with an unknown destination or an unclear path. That was me—showing up to school every day, doing just enough to get by, and living in the moment.

If viewed as a metaphorical journey, such as the captain of a sailboat at sea, I spent a significant amount of time simply wandering between the ebbs and flows of the ocean waves. I chose my path carelessly and without a clear destination. As my mother often said, "I went where the wind took me." So, what did this approach yield?

When I graduated from high school, my meandering strategy resulted in an unremarkable experience. Upon graduating, I had earned a 2.2 GPA. I was emotionally distraught after my high school girlfriend broke up with me, likely due to my lack of direction. My athletic career had come to an end, something that had consumed much of my time. Socially, the few friends I had went off to college, which left me spending time with acquaintances from work who had questionable ethics. My aimless lifestyle led me to a dark, lonely place, and it undoubtedly marked the lowest point of my life.

Right after high school, unsure of what to do next, I followed in my father's footsteps and took a job in a factory. I spent my days piling boxes in a shipping department. This monotonous routine, combined with my lack of direction, made each day feel like a cruel joke, repeating itself endlessly in mundanity.

After a year and a half, I decided to apply to college. I was fortunate and grateful that The Ohio State University offered me a much-needed opportunity. This break was essential for me, and I truly appreciated it. I began my studies in the winter of 1991, just a few days before my twenty-first birthday.

Just as I was beginning to improve my life—almost like a cosmic joke—I faced an unexpected challenge: stage IV cancer. The diagnosis was a tremendous shock at the time. I underwent intense chemotherapy and radiation treatments, but in the end, I found the event to be bittersweet. On one side, my body was beaten and battered. I was a shell of myself, having lost eighty pounds in the process. Yet, this confrontation with mortality brought me an unexpected moment of clarity and purpose. I learned that time was not meant to be wasted.

From the moment I walked out of the Arthur G. James Cancer Hospital in 1992, I committed myself to reaching the pinnacle of human achievement—or at least as high as my abilities could take me. I freed myself from the aimless behavior and self-doubt I had adopted and began to seek out the wise guidance and counsel of others.

INTRODUCTION

For much of human history, we have been told by parents, teachers, bosses, and society that as we grow more advanced, things get better. Such as, if we gain a better understanding of emotional health, we improve our ability to regulate our emotions. With the development of more communication methods, we become increasingly connected. This greater connectivity leads to a more civilized society. Throughout much of human history, this has been demonstrated to be true.

However, the fabric of this reality is beginning to fray.

Recent studies have shown a reverse correlation among several interconnected factors. Our intelligence quotients (IQ) are declining, emotional stability is worsening, and ethical decision-making is deteriorating. As a society, we are becoming increasingly antisocial, and our physical health is declining as well. It seems we may have reached a tipping point in human development.

Given these findings, I believe it is crucial for us to revisit and analyze the additional factors that have influenced this complex relationship between human growth and societal progress. If we choose to overlook these shifts, we will face significant consequences. Consider the implications if these declines were to persist. The human species would become increasingly ignorant, isolated, emotionally unstable, ethically compromised, and unhealthy. No doubt, a frightful future.

So, what is it that is causing these declines?

Believe it or not, modern conveniences may be leading us toward our slow and steady demise. What is most disturbing is that our advancements and comforts continue to increase. Over the past century, we have filled our homes with kitchen appliances, washers, dryers, telephones, and televisions. Our driveways are now populated with various vehicles. In the last twenty-five years, we have progressed to home computers, the internet, and smartphones. Recently, in the past decade, quantum computers and artificial intelligence have emerged, threatening to change our lives exponentially. Can you feel it? The momentum of advancement is accelerating at a pace that is barely discernible to us, and we are only just beginning to recognize the negative impacts of all these conveniences.

I am not advocating for eliminating these technologies but rather redefining the purpose of humankind. I believe we must first analyze the patterns that have caused this shift, evaluate their impact, and create a new pathway to ensure humans do not stagnate and unknowingly perpetuate our own demise.

PART I

THE FOUNDATIONS OF EMERGENCE

CHAPTER ONE

THE TRICOLON

The Magic of Three

Three Is a Magic Number
—Bob Dorough[1]

The "Magic of Three" refers to the idea of grouping items in threes. This theory posits that three is the minimum number of events needed to demonstrate a pattern. This process of reflection allows a person to first seek to understand, second to analyze and evaluate, and third, to decide. As an example, when I was contemplating taking on my first headship, I asked my head of school at the John Cooper School, Mike Maher, "Mike, when will I know if Valley School of Ligonier is the right fit for me?"

He paused for a moment before saying, "After three years, Jon. You will go through three stages: In the first year, you listen intently; in the second year, you learn; and in the third year, you lead. Trust me, you'll understand this by the end of the third year." He was right; those three years gave me the wisdom I needed to determine whether Valley School was a good fit for me and whether I was a good fit for the school.

As humans, we are naturally drawn to patterns. Over the past twenty-nine years, I have had the privilege of working in three exceptional schools: the Stanley Clark School in South Bend, Indiana (eleven years), the John Cooper School in The Woodlands, Texas (nine years), and the Valley School of Ligonier in Rector, Pennsylvania (nine years). Throughout this experience, I have been able to explore both the differences and the similarities that highlight what makes each of these schools unique. I present to you their current mission statements. I encourage you to pay attention to the differences and similarities.

The Stanley Clark School, established in 1958, is a PS–8 school with approximately 350 students. SCS is in a stable-growth suburban neighborhood. Stanley Clark was recognized as a Blue Ribbon School, the highest award an American school can achieve. The mission of the Stanley Clark School is:

> We inspire each student to find a joy of learning through a comprehensive journey rooted in excellence, igniting limitless potential.[2]

The John Cooper School, a K–12 institution established in 1988, has over 1,350 students enrolled. It is located in a rapidly growing suburban neighborhood and has a significant international student population. It was voted the Best Private School in The Woodlands, Texas, and fourth best in all of Texas.

> The John Cooper School is an independent, non-sectarian, co-educational, college preparatory day school. Our mission is to provide a challenging education in a caring environment to a diverse group of select students, enabling them to become critical and creative thinkers, effective communicators, responsible citizens and leaders, and lifelong learners.[3]

Valley School of Ligonier, founded in 1946, is a K–8 school that has recently achieved its highest enrollment with 225 students, despite a declining demographic in Westmoreland County, Pennsylvania. Nestled in a rural, natural setting, the school is surrounded by forests and a bubbling stream, enhancing its charming atmosphere. In 2023, Valley School was voted the best private school in Westmoreland County.

> In an environment that is safe, challenging, nurturing, and disciplined, Valley School provides a balanced and strong program of study for a diverse group of children. Our goal is to stimulate in each young person lifelong habits of moral behavior, seeking wisdom, and doing good works for others.[4]

The three educational institutions vary greatly in terms of race, religion, geography, age groups, enrollment size, cultural and political leanings, and historical background. These are all differentiating factors when considering school culture. Yet, despite these differences, it is important to point out that all three schools have managed to achieve educational exceptionality.

What, then, are the similarities that define their ability to succeed and ultimately foster Emergence? Let's first define Emergence.

EMERGENCE

The John Templeton Foundation defines emergence in this clear and concise way: "the distinct patterns and behaviors that can arise out of complex systems."[5]

As parents and educators, you likely recognize that raising and educating children are complex processes with many phases, milestones, and natural patterns of progress. It begins with the helplessness of infancy, when their caregivers are their entire world. Then come the energetic years of toddlerhood, when natural curiosity begins to take shape. During the preschool years, children learn to dress themselves and create pictures for you to display on the fridge, leading up to their first day of kindergarten. Adolescence introduces a whirlwind of physical changes, hormone fluctuations, and the capacity to argue about even the simplest matters, all part of their quest for independence—a necessary challenge, I suppose.

Yet, there is another element to Emergence—a more purposeful one. Emergence involves not only recognizing patterns within complex systems but also *structurally enhancing successful habits while simultaneously suppressing destructive habits*. So, how does one accomplish this, and what is the impact?

Nature may very well provide the answer.

Have you ever looked closely at a stalk of broccoli? Astonishingly, the structural pattern repeats over and over again—variously scaled versions of itself make up the whole. This phenomenon is called *self-similarity*, and you can also see it in shells, trees, rivers, coastlines, and mountains. It is nature's way of providing physical structural integrity to an ecosystem—a mathematical code embedded in the universe itself.

In Figure 1.1, I highlight a Sierpinski equilateral triangle based on the concept of self-similarity.

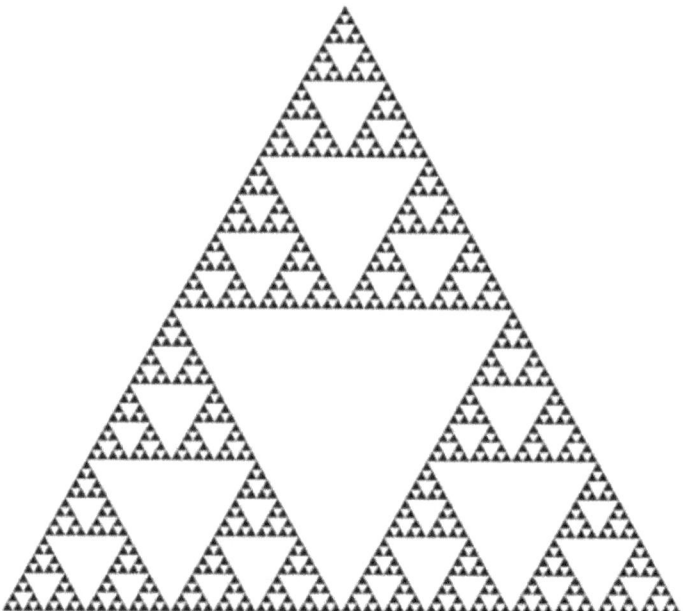

Figure 1.1. Sierpinski Triangle

So, how does this apply to a child's life? Fractals are repetitive features that create patterns that construct a framework that provides strength and stability to a system based on three elements: overall shape, repeating patterns, and adherence of bonds. If you look at the image above, this fractal set is built out of equilateral triangles and nothing more. No matter how close you get to the image, the pattern repeats infinitely. Nature utilizes this structural methodology because it creates a powerful foundation. As in our schools and life, children need a foundation of stability and strength to work from if they hope to reach Emergence.

Let's look at an example. Since I mentioned the fractal properties of broccoli, which, of course, all children love, we'll start with a child's physical health.

The condition of a child's physical health is directly related to their daily behaviors and consistency of activities. The more nutritiously they eat, the more they exercise, and the more restful their sleep, the better their cell function. The better their cell function, the more efficiently their organs remove waste and toxins and pump oxygen through the body. Additionally, beneficial cell function fosters electrical and chemical activity in the brain. The better the system performs, the more physically responsive they are.

Their bodies work like a fractal structure in which positive patterns build a self-reinforcing system of physical development and health. The whole is composed of the parts. You should consider what your children eat, their physical activity, and how well they rest. If you imagine each meal, each night of sleep, and each day of play as building a structurally sound triangle, what would your child's triangle look like?

Figure 1.1 provides one visual example:

Perfect Equilateral Triangles—A child remains active, eats right, and gets plenty of rest. From a natural point of view, a child's ability to achieve these three elements will create a framework of health and vitality, likely leading to a long life.

For a different example, see Figure 1.2:

Amorphous Triangles—Sedentary lifestyle, eating junk food, and staying up all night. Here, the child is not developing healthy habits in a consistent way. The triangle is misshapen and foundationally weak.

Figure 1.2. Amorphous Sierpinski Triangle

Whatever structure a child builds based on their individual behaviors will define them fundamentally. If a child develops properly, that structure should be seen as a solid foundation to continue to build upon. If they do not develop properly, you might hear the phrase, "I feel like my life is falling apart." Literally, this is the case. Our ability as schools and families to help young people develop these fractal habits is fundamental to their success.

When I consider Valley School's program in regard to physical health, children receive ample amounts of physical play outdoors, multiple recesses, regular gym classes, and classroom movement. They also receive nutritious lunches with homemade meals, a daily salad bar, and a combination of fruits, with an occasional dessert (not daily). We monitor such elements as salts, sugars, and carbohydrates. We also explain to our families the importance of sleep, including removing all distracting elements from a bedroom. This school/family partnership is vital to ensure proper sleep. Even the school nurse provides regular updates on regional and building sickness levels. This intentionality from the school and families ensures children experience a physically healthy environment in which to foster their habits.

In addition to their physical health, at Valley, we also consider a child's intellectual, social, emotional, and ethical intelligence with the same level of intensity, intentionality, and complexity. Each of these aspects plays a vital role in fostering a well-rounded child. Please refer to Figure 1.3 as a model of this holistic structure.

So why is it so hard for schools and families to perceive problems and solutions in this complex, structured way? It's because our evolutionary code has preprogrammed us to find fast, simple answers. Since the dawn of human civilization, humans have fought for survival. Long ago, our existence was predicated on our ability to fight off predators, freeze in place to remain unseen, and flee when necessary. We sheltered in caves, traveled for food, and joined collectively to ensure safety in numbers. For millennia, because our survival was so tenuous, our brains constantly reinforced fight, flight, or freeze responses.

It was appropriate and effective for the time, as we carved out a niche for our species in the intricate web of life. But human existence no longer works in this fashion. We have become so dominant that food is plentiful for most, we don't have to worry about predators, and heck, we even

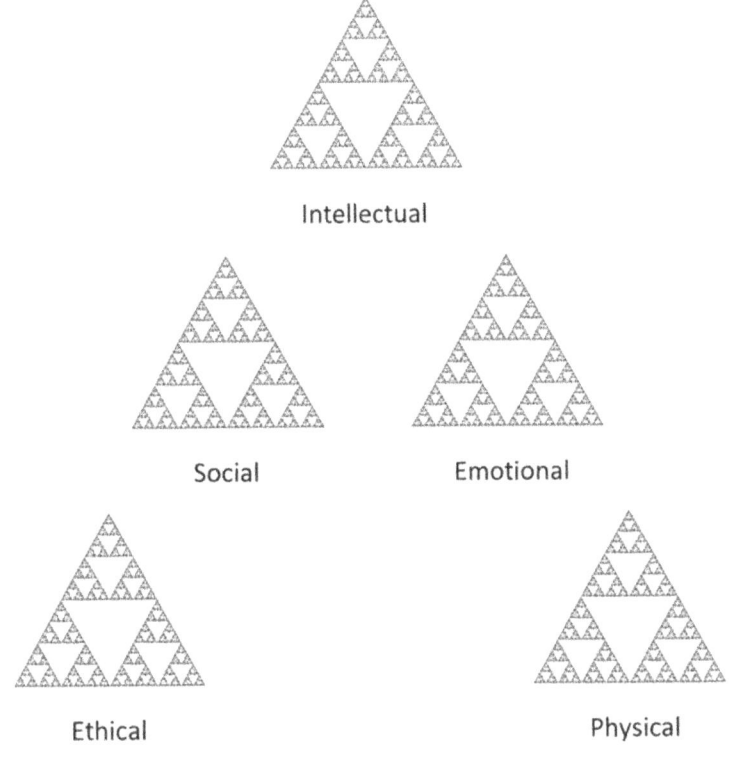

Figure 1.3. Five Intelligences

consider traveling into the wilds to be a form of recreation. Natural fears have morphed into artificial anxieties. This is one of the reasons we go to scary movies, read thriller novels, and participate in escape rooms. Those artificially induced fears produce a spike of adrenaline we enjoy, without the risks of actual danger.

It is essential to understand that complex thinking is necessary to produce meaningful and long-sustaining solutions. In high-stress moments, our biological impulses compel us to deactivate our high-level cognitive skills in favor of baser life-saving reactions. I am sure you see this regularly in your schools and your children when they don't appreciate your insights. They may lash out in a combative emotional tone (fight), stomp off in a huff (flight), or become incapable of engagement (freeze). These emotionally charged responses lead them to revert to simple solutions to complex problems. Unfortunately, simple solutions often result in more problems than they are intended to solve.

COMPLEX SOLUTIONS TO COMPLEX PROBLEMS

This information comes at a culturally critical time—a societal crossroads. The truth is that the world is on a slippery slope of decline. This assertion is not hyperbolic but rather based on countless statistical studies that I highlight in Chapter 2, as well as educational observations. As I mentioned previously, but it bears repeating, we have confirmed a significant decline in our five essential intelligences.

- Physical Intelligence: increased obesity, lack of sleep, and less nutrition
- Intellectual Intelligence: decreasing IQ scores and increased fragmented thinking
- Social Intelligence: increased isolation and antisocial behavior
- Emotional Intelligence: increased anxiety and depression
- Ethical Intelligence: increased personal gain and declining trust levels

The question is, how can individuals and schools combat these trends to positively impact society? First, we must acknowledge that complex thinking is essential for finding productive solutions. We need to prioritize fierce and civil conversations that require us to engage our intellect, consider social impacts, philosophize about solutions, practice empathy, and understand the physical ramifications of our actions. This approach will help us avoid being swayed by simplistic reactions and slogans that stem from our instinctual "fight, flight, or freeze" responses. By doing so, we can create a meaningful and positive impact in our schools, in our families, and in society at large.

CHAPTER TWO

A BLEAK FUTURE

Surviving an Era of Intrusive Convenience

> *A great civilization is not conquered from without*
> *until it has destroyed itself from within.*
> —WILL DURANT[1]

A CHILD'S WISH

Every winter at Valley School, the admissions director, division heads, head of finance and operations, and I meet with prospective parents. During these meetings, we emphasize the purpose of the visit, explain how to access our Tuition Within Reach program, and discuss our various educational offerings. I am fortunate to present our vision, mission, and core values. Our core values are centered on five key intelligences: intellectual, social, emotional, ethical, and physical development.

I particularly enjoy meeting the families of kindergarten students. They are eager for their children to begin their educational journeys, and their enthusiasm during the meeting is infectious. Their optimism is palpable, and they absorb information like a sponge. As they prepare to partner with us, I realize that they are entrusting us with their most precious gift: their children. Together, we embark on a journey of self-development, a responsibility we take very seriously.

During these meetings, parents often ask about several key themes: meeting intellectual potential, developing close and lasting friendships, exploring the natural environment, gaining self-confidence, and hoping their children grow into people of integrity. These are all admirable qualities. We assure parents that Valley School is committed to helping their child reach their potential, and begin the process of aligning them with the Valley Core Values: wisdom, wellness (mental and physical), integrity, and community.

For the youngest families entering school for the first time, this is about as far as their questions take them. However, there are older parents in the process as well who have experienced life outside of our school. Their questions allow us to delve into the complexity of past experiences.

Here is a segment of a personal conversation regarding their sixth-grade daughter, Amy, applying to Valley School.

> Dr. Strecker, Amy has given up. We don't know what to do. She says the work is too hard, she recently got into a fight with a classmate, and she cries most nights. When we asked her what she wanted, she told us she wanted a fresh start. I wish Valley School could help her.

I began the process with an optimistic and realistic conversation involving Amy, the division head, and her parents. I emphasized that she was at a crossroads, a point at which she may remain on a path of chaos or choose and seek a path of success. With tears in her eyes, Amy squeaked out the word "success."

For the next half hour, we discussed her past interactions. We wanted to know from Amy what was causing her chaos. Here is what she identified.

- To keep up, Amy used the internet to get by on homework—basically, using online programs to solve her academic problems. While she kept up with homework, she regularly failed the in-school tests.
- She got into a verbal argument over a topic on the news with another girl after watching a heated debate on TV the night before. The encounter ended with the girls shoving each other and suspensions.
- Amy wasn't sleeping well because she was surfing on social media sites late into the night. She had lied about her age to gain access. She admitted she was lonely.

Simply put, her foundation was misstructured, much like the graphic in Figure 2.1.

Amy had navigated her issues with quick-fix solutions as a result of lacking the needed wisdom to handle the situation adeptly. We began by

Figure 2.1. Amorphous Sierpinski Triangle

restructuring her home life and school life to provide the needed steps to help her become foundationally strong.

Amy was given access to multiple teachers, the school counselor, and the division head whenever she needed assistance. Additionally, we sent weekly updates to her parents to keep them informed. The parents agreed to take all technology away at night, and they monitored the computer during study time. To help her integrate socially, we arranged for her to befriend our most capable, empathetic, and ethical students, and we placed her in academic classes that matched her abilities. She embraced the program and made deep and lasting friendships.

I am happy to report that after Amy's successful two-year experience at Valley School, Amy has since graduated from a local university with high honors.

FRACTAL LEARNING

Why does Amy's story of struggle resonate with so many young people in today's culture? It really comes down to a lack of clear values and an overabundance of convenience. Let's go back to our triangle.

In a well-developed framework (see Figure 2.2), there are three elements of importance.

- First, it requires shape—For a school and families, it is the intentional core values. These values cannot be a poster you hang on the wall and forget about; they have to be ever present in a school and family's mind and actions. The values are the shape.
- Second, it requires repeated patterns—For a school and families, it is the day-to-day behaviors repeated consistently. That self-replicating pattern breeds stability and fit. Even in the smallest decision, the pattern will be repeated if based on the values.
- Third, it requires structural integrity. This is the mortar to cement these behaviors into place. For schools and families, these are the cultural and accepted bonds that hold the entire structure together.

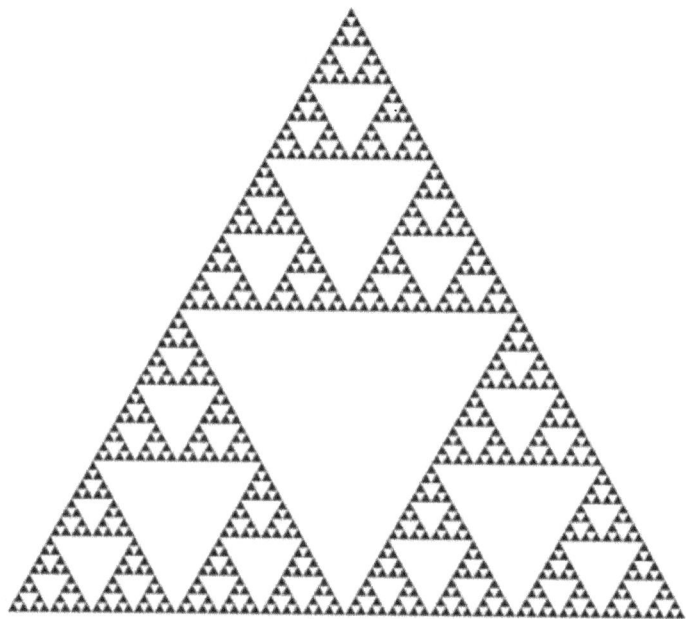

Figure 2.2. Sierpinski Triangle

Figure 2.3. Collapsing Structure

However, modern culture does not make this an easy endeavor. A society with an overabundance of convenience (plethora of choices, confused values, and lack of strength built out of adversity) is equivalent to multiple shapes, inconsistent patterns, and degrading mortar (see Figure 2.3). It may be in the shape of a triangle, but it is simply a facade.

Even the slightest bit of instability can collapse the structure entirely. In this situation, your children may seem well put together one day and fall apart the next.

RELATIONSHIP BETWEEN CONVENIENCE AND SELF-DEVELOPMENT

So why is this a recent phenomenon if we have been experiencing increased convenience for much of human existence?

In the past, there was a consistent positive correlation between convenience and self-development. As convenience increased, so did human development (see Figure 2.4).

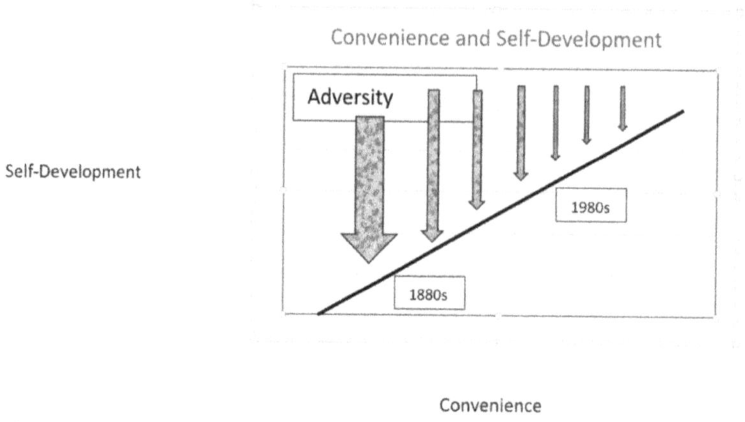

Figure 2.4. Relationship Between Convenience and Self-Development

The graph illustrates the relationship between convenience and self-development. As convenience increases on the x-axis, self-development also rises on the y-axis. Additionally, the graph highlights the role of adversity in fostering personal growth. When convenience is low, adversity is high, which can lead to stifled self-development when adversity is significant.

Imagine a child growing up in the early 1880s (see point on the graph), a time before mechanized equipment made daily tasks easier. Life was labor-intensive, with farm animals used to pull plows and transport goods. Farmers spent their days working in the sun, lifting, pulling, and toiling. Children were expected to help with farm life, often dropping out of school early, if they attended at all. Figure 2.4 illustrates the adversity faced by farming families. While the physical demands of farm work made the children stronger, the lifestyle limited their social and intellectual experiences. This doesn't mean they were dissatisfied with life; rather, their opportunities to reach their full human potential were constrained.

Let's fast forward to the 1980s (see point on the graph). With advancements in mechanization and technology, children were no longer limited to farm life. The barriers they faced were significantly reduced, allowing them to participate in school experiences. For many, this meant working before and after school, which helped them continue to build physical strength. Additionally, attending school provided opportunities for socialization, emotional support, participation in sports, adherence to the school's ethical expectations, and intellectual stimulation. As a result, these conveniences allowed children to access greater opportunities for personal development while still experiencing a healthy dose of adversity.

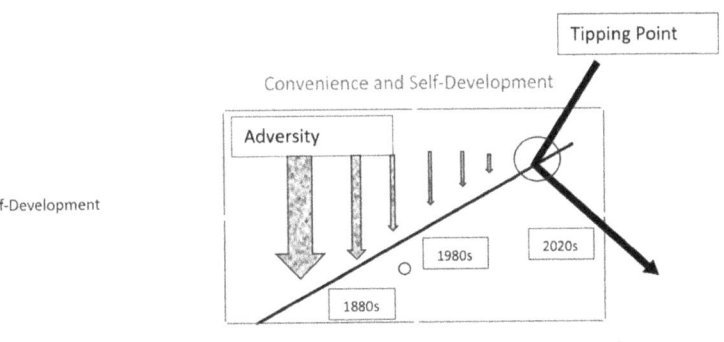

Figure 2.5. Relationship Between Convenience and Self-Development TP

But something has changed. The human condition is now in decline. That inflection point is the *Tipping Point*—a point at which there is no longer sufficient adversity to make children stronger so they are able to accomplish similar results as they grow weaker (see Figure 2.5).

Truth is, adversity has been reduced to the point of nonexistence unless intentionally focused upon. Many children only face significant physical adversity if they choose to participate in sports. Intellectually, new technologies allow children to simply input their questions into an AI program, and the work is done for them. The awkwardness of social interaction has been greatly reduced by simply swiping right or left on an app to find a date. Emotionally, we simply medicate our children to overcome their phobias and anxieties. Finally, culture has promoted an individualized-centric philosophy, abandoning the importance of social responsibility. The adversity that used to make children mentally and physically stronger has been reduced and children are unhappier, more lonely, less educated, overweight, and compromised.

You want proof—here it is.

Intellectual Decline

The Flynn Effect describes the consistent increase in intelligence test scores observed across generations, named after psychologist James R. Flynn, the scientist who studied this phenomenon extensively. Flynn noticed that IQ test scores grew progressively stronger over the course of fifty years. The graph (see Figure 2.6) shows that all subset tests exhibited an upward trajectory from 1954 to 2004. However, if one looks carefully, the pattern is not entirely linear. Starting in the 1970s, the progress began to lessen for a few of the tests.

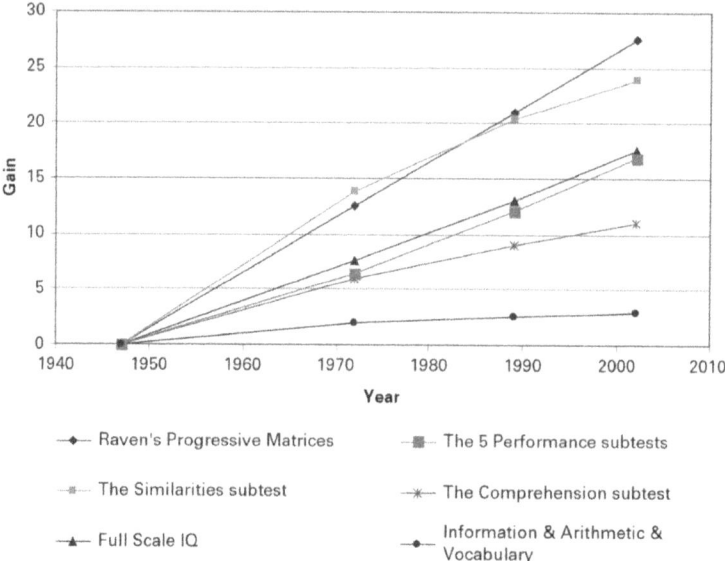

Figure 2.6. Flynn Effect

INTELLIGENCE QUOTIENT INCREASES—FLYNN EFFECT

Correspondingly in 2018, a study titled "The Flynn Effect in Norway and Other Countries: Practical Implications and Theoretical Questions," authored by Storsve, Sundet, Torjussen, and Lang-Ree, was published in the *Scandinavian Psychologist* and considered the Flynn Effect. The researchers found and highlighted anomalies based on the test scores of Norwegian recruits (see Figure 2.7).[2] Starting in the early 1990s, you began to see a downward trend in intelligence.

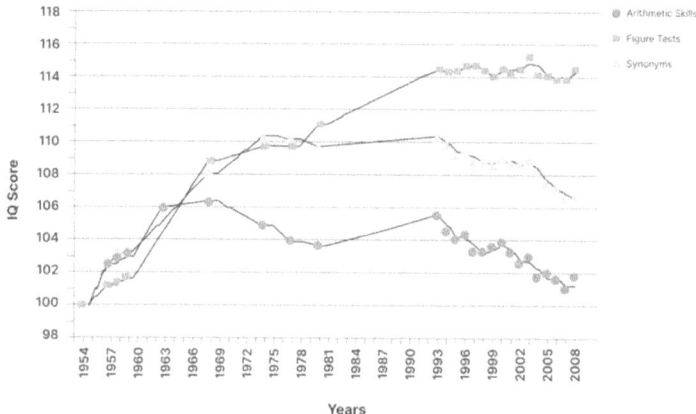

Figure 2.7. IQ Trends—Norwegian Recruits

INTELLECTUAL DECLINES

It is just recently that this downward trend is being considered in the United States. In an article in *Popular Mechanics* by Tim Newcomb, "American IQ Scores Have Rapidly Dropped, Proving the 'Reverse Flynn Effect,'" the author highlights a precipitous decline in human intelligence in the United States.[3] Much like in the Norwegian study, the declines are shown to have started in the 1990s. Much has been made of the reasons why—perhaps smart technologies, gaming, failing nutrition, faltering school systems, and social media. Regardless of the reasons, intellect is in decline. What about the other four intelligences, you ask?

Social Engagement Decline

The article "The Social Architecture of Impactful Communities" by Nick deWilde draws insights from Robert Putnam's book *Bowling Alone*; both the article and the book emphasize the decline in social engagement.[4] While there was a slight decrease in engagement from 1972 to 1985, a significant drop is evident from 1985 to the mid-1990s. This trend is illustrated in Figure 2.8, which shows that attendance at public meetings regarding town or school affairs, participation in clubs, involvement in committees, and the number of individuals interested in government affairs have all decreased over time.

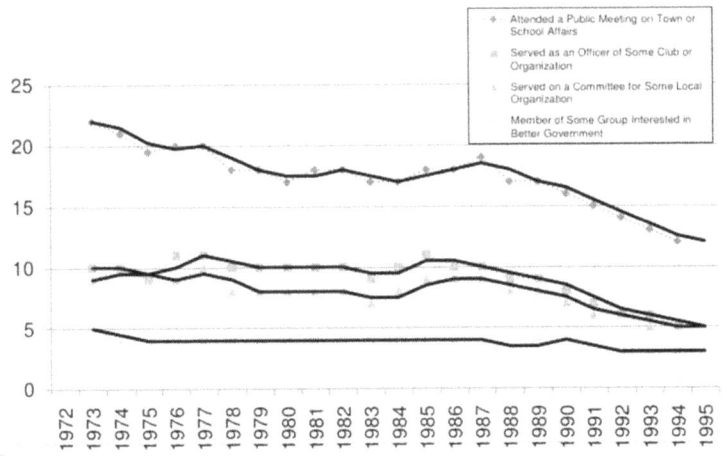

Figure 2.8. Declines in Social Engagement

Social/Emotional/Physical Declines

DailyMail.com published an article titled "Opioid Epidemic, Poor State of Healthcare and Increased Time Spent Online Are Making Us MISERABLE as America Drops a Place on the World Happiness Scale." The article highlights the decline in happiness, in-person social interaction, and sleep when compared to the number of hours spent online.[5] As expected, the data revealed an inverse relationship: As internet usage has increased, all three areas—happiness, social interaction, and sleep—have declined (see Figure 2.9).

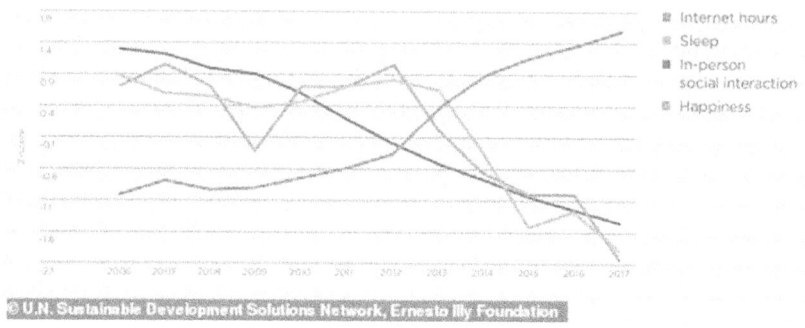

Figure 2.9. Declines in Sleep, Social Interaction, and Happiness

Trust Declines

Kevin Vallier, in his article, "US Social Trust Has Fallen 23 Points Since 1964," highlighted the downward shift in US social trust (Figure 2.10), indicating ethical concerns have grown more prominent over the last sixty years.[6]

So, why are we experiencing these multifaceted declines? Some may point to technological advancements, others to nutrition; some may suggest gaming, news media, educational decision-making, etc. Whatever the rationale, I believe it comes down to one fundamental reality: *CONVENIENCE*. Convenience of our mind, our bodies, and our social experiences. As convenience increases, adversity decreases.

The very tools we created and implemented to make life easier are the very factors contributing to our recent declines. We have reached, for the first time in human history, a cultural convenience tipping point.

It is not that convenience is objectively harmful, as we all benefit from and appreciate the ways in which conveniences ease our burdens, but when

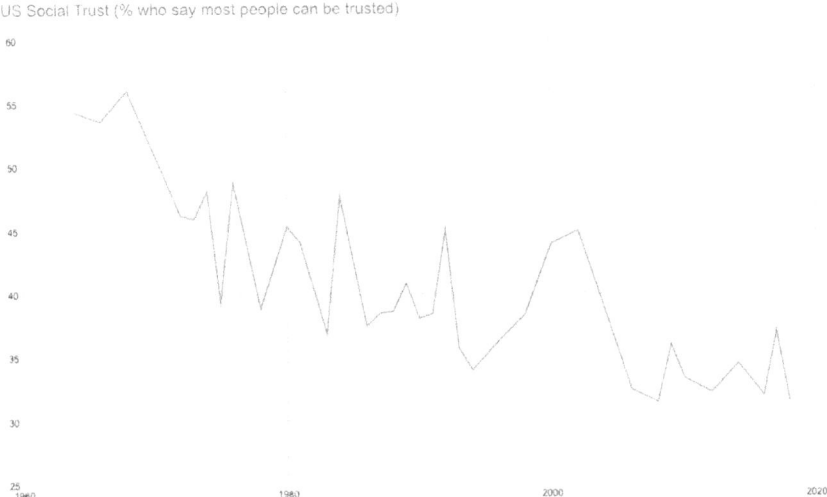

Figure 2.10. Trust Declines

we fail to purposefully manage the free time we are gifted by our countless conveniences, we risk succumbing to adding more work to our lives to pay for additional conveniences or, ironically, we allow apathy and languor to take root, as we mind-numbingly check out. Regardless, we feel busier than ever while accomplishing less.

Let's imagine a scenario—A Series of Unintended Convenience Consequences:

- A seventeen-year-old decides he wants a car as a convenience to get to soccer practice, but money is tight as a family. The parents agree to pay for an affordable car, but he has to pay for insurance.
- The young man gets an after-school job to help pay for the coverage.
- Things are going well until he realizes he doesn't have the adequate time he needs to study properly because of his job and sports schedule. His grades drop.
- He sees an online study program and thinks it is a good idea.
- He picks up a few extra hours at work to pay for the monthly subscription.
- The cycle continues—seeking convenience and adding work.
- Eventually, he drops sports because he doesn't have time for his studies, his job, and his athletic activities.

The very reason he wanted the convenience was to make it easier to enjoy athletics, and in the end, athletics was the thing he sacrificed. Have you ever felt that the things that you think might add convenience to your life are the very things that are causing you and your child anxiety?

How about the alternative response? We have become apt to fill our time with mind-numbing undertakings instead of enriching activities. Think about the convenience of the smartphone as a singular example. It is an all-in-one device. Think of its capacities—phone, computer, TV, global connector, gaming system, music player, etc. No matter what your interest, it sits in your pocket enabling you to frictionlessly fill every waking moment in the most addictive way possible. You can simply bounce from one activity to the next, always finding something to fill your time.

As an educator, it concerns me that children, when exposed to smart technologies, fill their available time with addictive habits and become increasingly socially disconnected, emotionally fragile, physically lazy, ethically compromised, and intellectually numb. Unless we manage these convenience tools, children will never reach their potential. But why do these conveniences do us so much damage? It all starts in our brains.

The human brain is an adaptive organ that builds upon itself as we learn. The more we learn, the more connections are formed. Simultaneously, in the interest of efficiency, the brain prunes unnecessary information. If we stop using memory to retain information, the brain removes the connection. When you consider the impact of convenience technologies, such as smartphones, we not only need to consider the benefits but also the negative impacts. For instance, phone numbers, schedules, directions, and general information are all embedded in our phones, available at a moment's notice, so we no longer need to memorize that information. As we're not using our informational memory with the same level of intensity that we did twenty, fifteen, or even ten years ago, our brains have severed these connections.

The process of retaining information in working memory and eventually shifting it to long-term memory is essential to connect memories. When a memory is placed into long-term storage, that information begins forming connections to other embedded memories.

Memory—phone number for Tom
Secondary memories—Tom's physical features, Tom's interests, Tom's wife's name (Sue).

The brain creates a lattice of memories to draw from.

However, if the information is only superficially held in short-term memory, much like notes scrawled on a Post-it note, the information will eventually be lost—either mislaid, lost in the daily shuffle, or intentionally tossed into the trash.

Artificial intelligence will create an even more consequential paradigm shift for humankind. I have used some of the newer technologies, such as AI photo editing, ChatGPT, Grammarly, and Revoicer with AI voice. They are, quite honestly, amazing. And also terrifying. If phones have taught us anything, it is that we must be intentional about setting ourselves up for success as new conveniences affect our lives. We must be ready to fill the gap productively created by these technologies. Otherwise, we run the risk of becoming intellectually complacent.

WHAT ELSE IS CONTRIBUTING TO OUR DECLINE?

While convenience technologies are a major contributor, they are not the only reason for our decline. Let's consider some of the research. A study by Norwegian researchers Bratsberg and Rogeberg concluded that men born after 1975 showed signs of intellectual decline as compared to those born before 1975. Rogeberg writes, "These environmental factors could include changes in the education system and media environment, nutrition, reading less and being online more."[7] The findings of this study have been validated by similar studies in Denmark, Britain, France, Finland, and Estonia, indicating that we should take these trends seriously. It is incumbent upon us to consider the reasons for intellectual decline and address the causes forthrightly.

Let's take a look at an example of how our modern world thwarts complex thinking, resulting in a failure to produce viable solutions to vital—and complex—problems. No one would deny that the combustion engine has made our lives more convenient. We all appreciate the benefits of getting from place to place easily via cars, trains, and planes. Thanks to the combustion engine, readily available goods and services are delivered to us within hours, the grocery store is abundant with options, and we have a plethora of clothing choices. It wasn't too long ago—before the combustion engine—that travel was arduous and dangerous, food and clothing were made mostly in the home, and it took months for goods to be delivered. All good things, right?

However, this convenience that has made our lives better and easier has also now caused travel congestion, pollution, and the warming of the earth. As life has become easier for humankind, there has been a cost to the health of our environment. Of course, there is no simple solution.

Simultaneously, we can also point to the polarity in the news media that makes us feel we must choose a side or diminish the need for comprehensive understanding, relying instead on insufficient sound bites. No matter the reason, both sides parrot simplistic talking points.

One side screams, "Drill, baby, drill!" and the other side pleads, "Just stop oil!" Both sides have good intentions; they want to ensure a better life for others. In simplistic terms, their efforts are admirable. Who doesn't want an easier life for their family and who doesn't want a beautiful planet on which to raise their children? These people with contrary opinions need to engage in a complex conversation rather than retreating to their polarized political and cultural corners preparing for the next round in their fight.

Reason for Educational Decline

Let's look at Bratsberg and Rogeberg's counterintuitive suggestion that modern education systems and policies have contributed to our intellectual decline. Certain changes in our American education system coincide with their timeline of intellectual decay. It makes you wonder whether educational reforms have contributed to Americans' diminished intellect. In 1983, the National Commission on Excellence in Education published a report that concluded that schools were failing: *A Nation at Risk: The Imperative for Educational Reform*.[8] As a result, President Bush and the US Congress established the No Child Left Behind Act (NCLB) in 2001, prioritizing improvements for disadvantaged children.[9] In simplistic terms, its objectives were benevolent.

However, the act also shifted our educational focus away from holistic development and toward test-oriented means of gauging success. Educators, now held accountable for children's test scores, began to modify their instruction and expectations accordingly, prioritizing teaching methods that would result in high test achievement instead of comprehensive development. This is not the fault of educators. If you tell teachers that they will be assessed on their students' test results, it should not be a surprise that the teachers do everything possible to produce the positive test scores you sought. This is another example of a well-intentioned but simplistic solution applied to a multifaceted, complex problem.

Teachers who have spent significant time in classrooms will tell you that the best way to maximize intellectual performance is to ensure children develop intellectual, social, emotional, ethical, and physical skills simultaneously. I am sorry to say that that is not what the NCLB Act advocated for, and those holistic skills were sacrificed as a result.

Education is near and dear to my heart. For the past twenty-eight years, I have worked in independent education, free from the constraints of the educational simplicity that government-imposed policy can create. Unbound by strict governmental rules, independent school educators are able to teach in a holistic style. That autonomy fosters academic success.

In many ways, I empathize with the teachers in the public education system. They entered the field for altruistic reasons. Educators commit to a life of helping young people achieve their full potential. Each day, they give of themselves fully for the betterment of others. Sadly, the system is flawed in ways that diminish teachers' efforts and create circumstances within which they cannot possibly achieve their intended results.

What is the difference?

All three independent schools I have worked in—and countless I have visited—have important factors in common:

1. Clear core values are centered on the intellectual, social, emotional, ethical, and physical growth of children. While the exact phrases, missions, and visions may differ, the overarching concepts remain the same.
2. A hierarchy of needs is prioritized. I will highlight these needs using Maslow's Hierarchy in Chapter 4.
3. Learning is achieved in its complete form. I will refer to Bloom's Taxonomy in Chapter 11 to reinforce this point.
4. There is no teaching to the test. Every child's academic success is measured based on their individual capacity to learn compared to their actual performance and progress. If a child is found to be underperforming, they receive the accommodations to bring them up to an expected level of excellence. This includes not only academic accommodations but also social, emotional, behavioral, and physical needs.
5. Expectations are never lowered. Convenience is not an option.

6. Faculty, staff, and administration work collaboratively to create complex solutions to complex problems. This requires additional time and energy, but the results are undeniable. In my current school, the vision, mission, and core values were created in partnership with members of the board, administration, parents, faculty, and staff.

To accomplish these important tenets of success, teachers in independent education tend to have increased planning time, fewer students per classroom, financially supported resources, and a voice at the table. Independent schools are typically smaller and, by extension, nimbler in the winds of change. In the end, both public and private educators want the best for children, but complex factors matter, and I feel our public school colleagues often work from a position of disadvantage.

News Media

Bratsberg and Rogeberg also highlight the effects of news media and social media. Let's tackle these items together. Consider television and online news reporting and political campaigns. They are quick to blame others or offer overly simplistic solutions. Please, no more short campaign slogans. The fear-based negativity this promotes can be maddening when you consider the effect on our mental health. The result is frustration, loneliness, depression, and anxiety, which drive us to question our own prosperity.

Young people are especially susceptible to this barrage of negativity, but they are not the only ones. Recent Harris Polls (2021 and 2023) highlight the following mental and physical health concerns.

- 83 percent of behavioral health workers worry there will be shortages in the workforce.
- 85 percent of Americans agree our nation faces a mental health crisis.
- 87 percent of Americans are concerned about the mental health of our youth.
- 50 percent of US parents with children under eighteen feel their children's mental health has suffered as a result of social media.
- 61 percent of adults have experienced undesired weight gain.
- Adults reported unwanted changes in sleep and alcohol consumption:
  - 67 percent reported non-desirable amounts of sleep.
  - 23 percent of adults drink more alcohol to cope with stress.[10]

I am dismayed to report that these statistics match my own personal observations as an educator and school administrator. As we all have been bombarded with sensationalized news in recent years, I have witnessed a greater occurrence of mental and physical sickness. Children, in particular, have developed an unwarranted fear of the dangers in society. We have adopted a "defend" mindset, sheltering ourselves from perceived harms, rather than the "discover" mindset that was so prominent in past generations and that encourages children to seek out new opportunities and experiences. This change in mindset was highlighted prominently in Jonathan Haidt's *The Anxious Generation*.[11]

So why do the media behave this way? Undeniably, our national media are influenced by advertising dollars associated with ratings. As a result, stories are sensationalized to keep viewers watching for the next segment. Cliffhanger after cliffhanger breed anxiety, and long-term exposure breeds depression. Media outlets neglect to give you the full story, and they consistently present editorial opinions as facts. It was once thought that the news media provided the checks and balances in society, keeping the government honest and the public informed. However, the media now seem to be an extension of the political parties' posturing to compel and maintain viewership.

In her article from *Mental Health News*, "Is Watching the News Bad for Your Mental Health? Staying Informed May Not Always Be Worth the Stress," Sara Lindberg highlights the negative impact of news on our thinking, behavior, and emotions.

> Consuming the news can activate the sympathetic nervous system, which causes your body to release stress hormones like cortisol and adrenaline. Then, when a crisis is happening, and we are experiencing this stress response more frequently, [Annie] Miller says physical symptoms may arise. Some of the most common symptoms are fatigue, anxiety, depression, and trouble sleeping.[12]

Believe it or not, the news media are providing convenience as well, as convenience of thought. Rather than presenting both sides of an argument to engage one's critical-thinking skills, they present information from a singular perspective, using simplicity like a cudgel to reinforce their echo chamber. Just remember, every convenience has an aftereffect, even the mental conveniences.

Social Media

The third area Bratsberg and Rogeberg identify is social media, which shares many characteristics of the national news media. It instigates stress and anxiety to activate your brain's emotional center and keep you engaged. However, there is another element of social media that underscores its nefarious intent: its convenience responsiveness. By observing what you say in front of your devices, what you click on—and worse—what you pause on while scrolling, the software learns what captures your attention and serves you more of it. I once paused on a cute beagle puppy video. I am still bombarded with those vivacious, long-eared puppers filling up my feed.

You might think, "So what? Just keep scrolling." But consider what happens to a person susceptible to anxiety and depression. In September 2017, I had a cardiac incident that almost ended my life. I went into cardiac arrest, and if not for some fast-acting doctors shocking me back to life, I would have died at the age of forty-seven. As you can imagine, I spent a lot of time afterward researching the potential outcomes and effects of a cardiac arrest. In no time, my feed was filled with all sorts of information about heart failure. Every twinge in my body felt like the beginning of another cardiac event. I was primed for stress, and social media fed the madness.

Luckily, my doctor suggested I stop my armchair research and avoid reading online about heart issues. It was the advice I needed to take control of my mental and physical health. I purchased a blood pressure monitor, a watch with an ECG reader, and a blood oxygen monitor. I started being attentive to real data taken from my body instead of convenient information online, some of which felt as though it were custom designed to provoke my anxiety. As a result of stepping away from the endless fear feed, my mental health, physical health, and intellectual performance improved.

Many of us believe that it is impossible—as individuals or collectively—to hold large profit-minded companies accountable for their part in our nation's mental health crisis. We feel powerless to solve our media-related problem at their source. Sadly, we are left to deal with the symptoms.

THE IMPORTANCE OF MINDSET

We have touched on a handful of external factors that contribute to intellectual and emotional declines in our schools and our children. Education, the impact of convenience, news outlets, and social media are only a few of the constraints that impede Emergence, and unfortunately, you have limited capacity to control them. However, the impediment we'll discuss next is within your control, and therefore, it's by far the most important. Do any of these phrases sound familiar?

> "I'm just not smart enough."
> "It is too hard."
> "I'm not a math person."
> "I've never been a good reader."
> "I don't know what to say."
> "I am not comfortable speaking publicly."
> "I can't handle it."
> "I'll just text."
> "I will fail."
> "I can't do it."
> "I don't deserve it anyway."
> "I do what I want when I want."
> "It's their problem."
> "I'm stupid."
> "It's good to be bad."
> "No big deal, no one will know."
> "I'll work out tomorrow."
> "It's only a few drinks."
> "Smoking a little weed won't hurt me."

These are the words of those who may have resigned themselves to the fact that they are destined for a mediocre life—possibly your students or your children. You may have even used some of these words yourself at times. Resorting to self-defeating thoughts is an understandable impulse in a world filled with adversity, yet it is not particularly helpful.

So first, let's eliminate some bad habits that may be affecting you and those you support. As children verbalize their reluctant state of mind with self-limiting statements, they are wiring a defeatist mindset to their emotional center. So, when they later face similar events, their brains will be emotionally conditioned to approach challenging events with hesitancy or cynicism. Now, if they eliminate these negative statements and replace them with optimistic affirmations, their brain will be rewired to face challenges from a constructive mindset.

Children also need to focus on those with whom they interact. If their family, friends, students, colleagues, or acquaintances have a propensity to minimize complex events, they might hear things like, "Oh, it's not a big deal," or "Fake it until you make it." These simple solutions, especially when dealing with complex problems, are insufficient. These people are authentically trying to be helpful; however, this kind of reductionist philosophy stymies emergent thinking in children.

We understand the emotional reason for it: to help children cope and feel better in the moment. However, there is a significant cost to negative self-talk and absorbing overly simplistic advice from others. First, it reinforces a negative mindset. Second, it dismisses the problem rather than solving it. Like an anchor on a ship, these words slow a child's progress or fix the child in place. It creates a state of mind that prevents children from developing into the complex thinkers they want to become. As a result, the distance between their reality and the person they aspire to be can seem vast.

Your students and children might say, "But other people have it so much easier."

Yes, we frequently run into people who seem to have everything together. It is almost as if they magically manifest their success with minimal effort. The Midas touch, if you will. But much like others' Facebook accounts are curated to present only the most covetable aspects of a person's life—vacations, eating in fancy restaurants, stunning home renovations, and not the dirty clothes heaped on the laundry room floor *after* vacation, the drive-thru meals or cooking failures, and the dust and disorder of home construction—in real life, too, we only see what others are willing to reveal. We don't hear or see the whole story. We tend to measure success by comparing ourselves to the best versions of others rather than evaluating our own progress. Children need to understand this completely, especially before they enter the virtual world.

This mindset reminds me of the 1982 song, "What About Me" by Moving Pictures. I have always loved the song, but I detest the defeatist chorus line as the band sings, "I want my share."[13]

Life isn't fair. That is the hard truth. You cannot simply shout out what you want and blame someone else when you do not get it. If you want "your share," you must become the best version of yourself. This level of achievement requires diligence, starting with rejecting the apparatuses that bind you to a defeatist mindset.

SUMMARY

- When you are offered convenience in life, recognize that you are simultaneously being offered unutilized time and unexpended energy. Work to intentionally fill that saved time with more complex intellectual, social, emotional, ethical, and physical tasks. Beware of wasting it with time-consuming and meaningless activities that can cause brain rot, such as doom scrolling, TV bingeing, and internet surfing.
- Be cautious when people offer you overly simplistic solutions to complex problems. It may feel good to have taken action quickly, but effective solutions have complex foundations and frameworks, so you may be wasting your time.
- As you seek to self-develop, consider the negative self-talk you are using to cope with your situation. Learn to recognize and remove these phrases from your vocabulary. Once mastered, you will adeptly recognize when others are in a defeatist mindset too. You may choose to help them think more positively about their potential. However, when providing advice to others, even with positive intentions, we can cause more problems if we don't consider the situation through a complex lens.

CHAPTER THREE

THRIVING IN COMPLEXITY

Grappling with Order and Chaos

Simplicity before understanding complexity is ignorance.
Simplicity after understanding complexity is genius.
—JAMES CLEAR[1]

Someone asked me why I didn't name this book *The Simplicity of Success*. Writing a catchy phrase to make it appear "easy to do" might lead to more book sales. However, there is no magic pill or wave of a wand that will lead your students or children to the type of success they seek. There is only an intricate way of looking at a chaotic world that will provide them with the answers they need. To be frank, simplicity is just too simple.

As I mentioned above, the decline in our society is directly related to our thirst for convenience and quick fixes. Simplicity is like an addictive drug; it feels good because it produces immediate—albeit superficial—results. Unfortunately, simplistic thinking and decision-making only mask the issues that must be thoroughly assuaged to achieve long-term success. Ultimately, simplicity dulls the senses. You can see it in all aspects of life. As physical labor becomes simpler, our overall fitness has suffered. As technology has improved and reduced our need to memorize and process information quickly, our intellect has decreased. This is true for social skills, emotional stability, and moral decision-making as well.

Simplistic ideas also lead to echo chambers, as they reject the validity of a broad variety of perspectives. It is black-and-white thinking. This perpetuates bias and encourages irrational opinions.

I observe that many young adults today tend to challenge rational thinking quickly and are often eager to silence informed speakers with whom they disagree. This behavior creates a harmful dynamic for both our society and personal relationships. Sadly, this reactiveness is sometimes supported by well-meaning but misguided educational professionals. It is essential that we resist this simplistic and narrow-minded ideology. Schools and parents should prioritize teaching children how to engage in civil discourse and demonstrate decorum, rather than simply telling them what to think. This includes developing the ability to listen intently and open-mindedly, which will encourage young adults to express their views thoughtfully, reasonably, and respectfully.

You may decide I am an old curmudgeon, a relic from a bygone era. I admit that I am a Gen Xer. Still, given the research I've highlighted, I feel justified in saying I worry about the future. Never in our history have we seen this level of societal deterioration in both scope and depth.

We exacerbate the situation when, rather than slowing down as a society to consider more complex solutions, we promote a frantic pace of life that forces us into superficial decision-making. This tendency leads to a sense of inadequacy because we can't keep up, or, as the students say, we experience "FOMO" (fear of missing out). As children attempt to process the abundance of intellectual information, social happenings, emotional postings, ethical debates, and body image expectations, it is nearly impossible for a child to feel healthy and connected. This is all to say that we are on a cultural collision course toward madness, and it's only speeding up.

ELLIOT: AN EXAMPLE OF SIMPLISTIC ADVICE

Let me share a funny and heartwarming story that perfectly captures the problem with simplicity. It's about a former middle school student, "Elliot." I was teaching an elective in general psychology. I felt that children could be successful holistically if they understood the basics of social interaction.

I suspected Elliot might be on the autism spectrum. He had difficulty maintaining friendships, struggled to communicate, and exhibited compulsive behaviors. But his symptoms were mild, and he was of gifted intelligence. While teaching this class, Elliot stayed afterward and asked if he could talk to me.

"Dr. Strecker, may I ask you a question?"

I replied, "Of course, Elliot."

He averted his gaze and said, "You explained some things about social interaction today in class, and I was wondering if they might work for me."

I replied, "Elliot, human dynamics come down to making connections like asking questions, listening intently, and providing positive physical feedback."

"Like what?" Elliot asked.

"Like looking me in the eye while you ask me a question for a start," I replied.

We stayed after class for the next few weeks to discuss techniques and strategies. He was so committed that he gave up his recess and study hall time. He was making steady progress, but his actions seemed forced and unnatural. You could sense he understood my recommendations intellectually but had to make a conscious effort to interact. He stuck with it. I was so proud of him.

A few weeks later, I got a call from the band teacher. He said that Elliot had made a poor choice at the band festival that weekend, and he wanted me to speak with him on Monday. When I asked for details, the band teacher said, "I can hardly believe it, but Elliot was kissing a girl from another school."

"What? Is this the same Elliot who hardly talks to anyone outside his closest friends?" I asked.

The band teacher said, "I wouldn't believe it if I hadn't seen it with my own two eyes."

"I will meet with him on Monday." I hung up the phone, more perplexed than disappointed.

On Monday, I called Elliot to my office, preparing to levy a consequence for his behavior, but before I did, I wanted to hear his side of the story.

Elliot arrived, head down, and slumped into one of my chairs. "Am I in trouble?"

After I explained the importance of representing our school in the highest regard and doing the right thing, I asked, "So, what happened?"

Elliot looked up at me, an enormous smile grew upon his face, and said, "Dr. Strecker, I followed all your advice. I looked her in the eyes. I asked questions rather than talking about myself. I smiled to let her know I was friendly, and the next thing I knew, she kissed me. So, I kissed her back."

Oh no, I thought, *this is my fault*. I contemplated my next step when he interrupted my thoughts and said, "Dr. Strecker, it was the greatest day of my life." He was gazing upward as if witnessing heaven itself as his hands were cupped over his heart.

I stifled a laugh and said, "Elliot, I didn't teach you everything. Let's talk about integrity at school events."

After considering the results of my actions, I realized that even the best intentions can cause problems if proposed as simple, solitary solutions. The world is complicated, and teaching children must take its complexity into account. A clear vision, mission, and core values are essential to healthy and holistic development for both individuals and societies; we mustn't rely on slogans.

If I were to go back and revisit my attempt to support the students, I would have offered a class on bringing about Emergence in a holistic capacity.

Take a moment to reflect on your life and its complexity. Consider the difficulties at your school or in raising your children. Do you find these problems easy to solve? No rational person would claim to have a simple fix to these dynamic problems.

For the sake of illustration, let's combine some issues simultaneously:

Imagine you are a single parent struggling to raise a family on too small an income. The refrigerator is empty and rent is due, so you may need to do some extra shifts at work. One night, you get a call from the teacher suggesting your child is not doing well academically and needs tutoring. Your child comes home to tell you he is lonely and being bullied by a former friend and wants to spend more time with you. Your boss asks if you can stay for some overtime this weekend. You could use the money for essentials and tutoring, but you hate working on Saturdays and Sundays because it is time away from your child, and the weekend manager keeps asking you out for a date.

This situation and many like it demonstrate the complexities of our daily dilemmas. What would you suggest the person address first? Which element is most important? It's difficult, isn't it? There is no "right" answer. Indeed, each element impacts the others to compound the challenges this parent faces, which causes a negative feedback loop.

Now, add in the complexities of our individualized characteristics. Our genetics, cultural experiences, family dynamics, educational opportunities, intelligence, levels of introversion and extroversion, emotional stability, ethical realities, and physical traits shape the situations we encounter and how we deal with them. They make us unique, but they also add to the complexity.

Reducing multifaceted scenarios like this one to a problem that can be solved with a handy five-step process oversimplifies the situation, leading only to disappointment and frustration.

HOW TO THINK ABOUT COMPLEXITY

In 2001, the movie *A Beautiful Mind* was released.[2] It is about the mathematician John Nash, a Nobel laureate in economics, who in the movie is played by Russell Crowe. John Nash was most famous for his work in Game Theory. After watching the movie, I was instantly inspired by his work. In particular, it was the bar scene that captivated me.

John Nash sits at a bar table with his mathematical papers in hand. A beautiful, tall blonde walks in with four friends. Nash's classmates, who are milling around, suddenly surround Nash and tell him to look up. When he does, he immediately notices the blonde girl. It is clear they are all interested in her. As the young men joke about future weddings and duels, his classmate, Hansen, played by Josh Lucas, says, "Have you remembered nothing? Recall the lessons of Adam Smith, father of modern economics."

The young men, in unison, recite Smith's teaching, "In competition, individual ambitions serve the common good."

The blonde immediately begins looking at Nash. Hansen notices the blonde's fixation on Nash and states, "He may have the upper hand now, but wait until he opens his mouth."

Looking directly at the blonde, Nash enters a daydream state and says, "Adam Smith needs revision."

Nash walks his classmates through the possible imaginary scenarios.

First, each one tries his luck by approaching the blonde. They strike out individually as they create a chaotic situation for her. Too many choices. She chooses none of them. Strike one.

Second, the young men approach the other four friends after approaching the blonde. Each advance is thwarted because no one likes to be chosen second. Strike two.

Nash advances a third idea: everyone simultaneously does what's best for themselves *and* the group. The blonde is then seen standing alone as the alpha female, and each young man is dancing with one of her friends. They each ignored the blonde to ensure the success of the group. This is one of the fundamental principles of complexity.

This example represents a complex solution to a complex interaction. It is simple to only worry about yourself in these situations, but planning a team strategy to ensure everyone has a good experience requires thoughtful design, timing, and teamwork. If people considered others' triumphs as part of their own definition of success, we would obtain a lot more victories individually—and collectively.

I encourage you to watch this scene on YouTube. I promise you it will be worth the three minutes of your time. It is a wonderful example of shifting from simplistic to complex thinking.

ACTIVE COMPLEXITY

Complexity: The Emerging Science at the Edge of Order and Chaos by Dr. M. Mitchell Waldrop is one of the most influential books I have read.[3] It is a fascinating journey into the science of order, complexity, and chaos.

The book describes the struggles and successes of the scientists when considering the intricacies of complexity science. I was astonished by the scope and depth of what I read. The clarity used to describe complexity within economics, biology, and computer science reinforced my belief that we can apply this methodology to human development.

Of all the charts I have studied, based on the work of Steven Wolfram, "The Edge of Chaos" presented by Waldrop most altered my conception of complexity. In Langton's work on "artificial life," he discovered that both chaos and order are required to develop a healthy and prosperous system, which suggests that a system flourishes on the "Edge of Chaos." This area (IV on the chart; see Figure 3.1) is where we must focus to promote Emergence within our children.

It is essential to understand that excessive uncertainty in a system can lead to overwhelming chaos, while too much control may result in stagnation. Let's examine a real-world example.

Mr. White runs his classroom with absolute authority. Mr. White expects pure order—a well-oiled, math-teaching machine. Everyone does their work, turns it in, and leaves the class without time for collaboration, small talk, or relaxing. As an example, if someone needs to use the

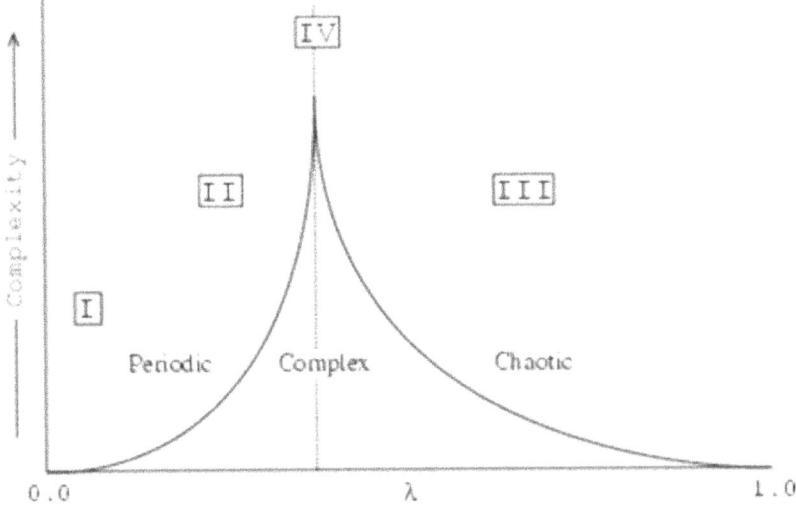

Figure 3.1. Edge of Chaos

restroom during Mr. White's class, they must click a time clock before leaving. This ensures the students don't abuse their bathroom breaks. Any violation is recorded. Note that this is a true story, although the details have been changed!

Mrs. Red's math class is just down the hall and runs on a different philosophy. Everyone does whatever they want. Mrs. Red preaches pure autonomy. She tells her students to come in when they want, take a break when they need one, and leave according to their own desires.

Which methodology will work, and which will not? Based on the "Edge of Chaos" theory, the reality is that they both will fail miserably.

Mr. White's students will suffer stagnation. The stifled students will become bored and resentful.

The students in Mrs. Red's class will be confused and disordered.

Individuals work best in a system with both enough chaos (freedom) available to maximize their development and foster trust and enough order (structure) to ensure efficient teamwork and growth. If either is overemphasized, the result will be stagnation (too much order) or chaos (too much disorder).

We all know parents and schools with too much order. I am sure you have met people and administrators who try to plan out everything. They think the more procedures and policies, the better. Heck, you may be one of them. Just know that too much order can dampen people's spirit and creativity, causing bitterness and a lack of productivity.

Think of the unyieldingly strict and orderly state in George Orwell's book, *1984*.[4] The dystopian novel is set in Oceania, a totalitarian society ruled by the Inner Party and its leader, Big Brother. The story follows Winston Smith, a member of the Outer Party, who, like all Outer Party members, lives under constant surveillance and the expectation of complete loyalty and submission to the Inner Party and its ideologies. Deprived of all personal freedom, Outer Party members live sterile, uncreative, unrewarding lives. Robbed of even opportunities to contribute to their society in ways that have not been prescribed for them by the Inner Party, members of the Outer Party are powerless, unambitious, frustrated, and disillusioned. When Winston boldly begins to rebel against the regime's oppression, he is captured and subjected to the Inner Party's brutal control. According to the "Edge of Chaos" model, no one could flourish in this type of environment. Orwell masterfully depicts the failure of applying too much control, which is the *only possible outcome* of the oppression that is the status quo in Oceania.

On the opposite end of the spectrum, we find systems that are too chaotic.

In Cormac McCarthy's *The Road*, the pervasive chaos of a postapocalyptic world profoundly impacts the characters and themes within the narrative.[5] The desolation surrounding the man and his son symbolizes the collapse of civilization, where the remnants of humanity have succumbed to brutality and despair. This chaos creates an atmosphere of constant danger, forcing the pair to navigate a landscape devoid of societal norms and filled with moral ambiguity. Their struggle for survival becomes a poignant exploration of hope in the face of annihilation, as they cling to their bond in a world where chaos breeds a moral vacuum. The father and son's journey illustrates the resilience of love and the human spirit, serving as a stark contrast to the chaos that threatens to engulf them, ultimately questioning whether remnants of kindness can endure amid widespread ruin.

So how do we find the right balance?

THE BOX SYSTEM: STRIKING A BALANCE BETWEEN ORDER AND CHAOS

Let me introduce the *Box System* (see Figure 3.2). Within the box, imagine a chaotic system running rampant. The elements inside the box (chaos)

Figure 3.2. Box System

bounce back and forth off its walls, testing its structural integrity. However, the walls of the box, which represent the mission, vision, and core values (controls) of your family or school, hold strong. Your ability to make the box bigger or smaller will determine your ability to bring about emergence, the act of procuring a desired result.

Consider a middle school dance. If you ever want to witness chaos, agree to chaperone one. The goal is multifaceted. You want to offer a social event where children can apply their social skills, remain emotionally regulated, behave appropriately, experience physical activity, and hopefully learn about the nuances of human dynamics. Let's imagine dropping that dance into the box.

For demonstration purposes, let's imagine we enlarge the box to total capacity (total chaos). There are no restrictions on the type of music, dancing, dress, or behavior. My goodness, I am getting heart palpitations just considering the pandemonium. As you can imagine, things would likely get out of control quickly.

Now, imagine the opposite approach. We squeeze the box down as tightly as possible (total control). We only allow classical music, balloons are taped to the stomachs of the middle schoolers to ensure they don't get too close, and the dress code is restricted to only suits and floor-length dresses. The children would likely rebel and wouldn't even bother coming to the next dance.

Neither scenario would result in the desired goals.

Now, let's use the Box System to maximize compliance and enjoyment. Herein lies its power. You can loosen or tighten the box based on the children's past behavior. If you have a group of particularly well-behaved children, you give them more autonomy to navigate the space. This allows them to mature successfully. A good time is had by one and all.

If the group is a little unpredictable and has some rogue elements, you can tighten the box to add order. Understand that the purpose is not to control every aspect of the dance, but to bring about enough stability to encourage Emergence. You want the children to enjoy themselves while meeting expectations. The children remain respectful and orderly but still mature socially as a result of the degree of autonomy they experience.

You should base the constraints (order) of *your* box on the vision and core values of your family or school while giving yourself enough freedom (chaos) to grow within them. If you manage the situation deftly, you will strike the balance at which you develop and maintain your core values, respond constructively to unexpected variables, and nurture the highest levels of understanding and complexity. The box and its contents are dynamic, so you can continuously adapt them to your learning, needs, and values.

SUMMARY

- Find collective and individual win-win scenarios, especially in education.
- It is important to move from a simplicity to a complexity mindset as we live in a complex world
- System optimization and Emergence live on the edge of order and chaos.
- To most effectively bring about Emergence, use the Box System, using both autonomy and order as your guides.

CHAPTER FOUR

PRIVILEGES AND DISADVANTAGES

Helping Children Understand and Overcome Their Initial Conditions

> *In Chaos Theory, the Butterfly Effect is the sensitive dependence on initial conditions, where a small change at one place can result in large differences in a later state.*
> —IAN MALCOLM (IN *JURASSIC PARK*)[1]

In the last chapter, I referenced the differences in life experiences. While I acknowledge that some may have it easier, there are certain realities that often go underappreciated when you begin from behind. This chapter highlights these differences.

Some are born physically beautiful or intelligent; others are naturally charismatic, confident, or exhibit honorable convictions. It is like hitting the genetic lottery. Others start in a less fortunate position. Some are less attractive, have a learning disability, or are overly shy. We all set out on a similar journey, but we don't all start in the same place.

It is important to understand your children's and students' initial conditions. This reality allows you to focus your efforts on their most important needs. For instance, if they don't have enough food to eat, it will prove extremely difficult for them to become actualized. Let me provide an example so you can consider how initial conditions affect a person.

I grew up in a small town. I was one of five siblings with two older sisters, Angie and Heather, and two younger brothers, Matt and Mark. My father worked in a factory, and my mother worked as a teller at a bank. I grew up in a small house (less than two thousand square feet for seven of us) in a close-knit neighborhood. The local park was just a block away.

If one were to analyze my initial conditions superficially, one might say that I was privileged to have both parents in the household and siblings for support. Others may point to neither of my parents having graduated from college as a disadvantage, given our financial reality. Both would be true. The reality is that all of us experience initial disadvantages *and* privileges.

Let's look at the pros and cons of my situation.

Pros: Two-parent household, siblings, friends, safe neighborhood, local park just down the street.

Cons: Latchkey home, finite financial resources for five children, little diversity in town.

Now, consider your own beginnings while you consider your students' or child's initial conditions.

- Where did you grow up?
- What sort of family do you have?
- Did you feel safe in your neighborhood?
- Did you have a collection of readily available friends?
- Were finances tight?

While it is important to recognize disadvantages and privileges, it is equally essential to avoid being defined by them. I have seen people raise themselves from the ashes of disadvantage with unrelenting will. I have also seen those who seemingly have everything working in their favor collapse under the pressure of abundance. Where a journey begins is not as critical as where it ends. Evaluating initial conditions is a wise first step because it tells you where to apply effort. However, assuming that you fully comprehend other people's initial conditions is reckless because an individual's situation can only be understood in the context of their whole truth.

Practicing restraint when judging others becomes pivotal when considering multiple factors: socioeconomic status, race, religion, age, mental and physical ability, gender, health, sexual orientation, and ethnicity. It is nearly impossible to create a hierarchical list of privileges and disadvantages.

In one breath, I could tell you I am a mid-fifties white male, six feet six inches tall, and married. I have a doctoral degree, am a professing Christian, and am labeled upper class. There is no doubt I have clear and present advantages and privileges now. As a result, people might make assumptions about my start in life, such as, "I bet you made straight A's, had an easy life, came from wealth, and went to a prestigious college."

However, in the same breath, I could tell you my initial conditions consisted of academic hardship (I failed second grade because I couldn't read), and I graduated high school with a GPA of 2.2. We didn't have the funds as a family for much extra beyond the basics, so I started working when I was sixteen. I worked in a factory before college and I was diagnosed with stage IV cancer at the age of twenty-one.

So, the full picture is more complicated than a list of demographic factors. I know the impact of disadvantage, and equally, I know privilege. Disadvantages are real and genuinely affect children trying to better their situations. They create more difficult journeys, but that doesn't mean that pathways to success do not exist for them. It can be hard to see one's own privilege when they are living in it. However, as one earnestly assesses initial conditions, if one finds oneself in a position of privilege, one should strive to help those struggling with disadvantage.

Here is another important perspective many do not fully appreciate. Starting from behind makes life more difficult for a child, no doubt. Their reality consists of a series of obstacles. As a result, they may feel like the world is screaming for them to abandon all hope and accept what appears to be a mediocre life laid out before them, while others have success and fulfillment within reach from the very start. But that amount of privilege does not always work to their advantage.

Famed college and NFL coach Barry Switzer once mused over those who are born into advantageous conditions. "Some people are born on third base and go through life thinking they hit a triple."[2] But have you ever met a person who seems to have everything working in their favor? They are born into a wealthy, two-parent household. They are intellectually and physically gifted (star athlete and honor roll student). They do everything right because, quite honestly, all their basic needs are satisfied. I have seen many of these types of students over the years, and while you might envy them at first glance, I worry for them from an educational point of view. Indeed, I feel sorry for them. It may seem counterintuitive to think this way, but their initial conditions often preclude them from developing vital attributes only nurtured through an arduous learning process. Being good at something can be a deterrent to becoming great at it. Sometimes, the only way to develop complex attributes is through continuous, strenuous effort and building resilience through adversity. Switzer might say that people with privilege may never even learn how to hit a ball.

But for those who must struggle to overcome challenging initial conditions, under all that excruciating pain lies the opportunity to develop life's most defining and valuable skills: determination, perseverance, grit, and resilience. These vital attributes are often unknown to those born with plentiful natural and circumstantial advantages. All five intelligences, developed through the lessons hardship can offer, will be to a person's advantage as they work to bring about their emergence.

Let me provide a visual.

In Figure 4.1, some might initially say the boy on the right has it much easier. That is true. But what often goes unnoticed is that the boy on the

Figure 4.1. The Inequitable Climb

left, to climb the steps, is growing stronger, smarter, and more confident. Eventually, those money stacks run out and both boys need to climb the remainder of the unseen steps. The boy on the right will be ill equipped for the challenge, whereas the boy on the left has honed his mind, body, and spirit for the challenges ahead.

MASLOW'S HIERARCHY OF NEEDS: A FRAMEWORK FOR REFLECTION

In 1943, American psychologist Abraham Maslow published a groundbreaking paper titled "A Theory of Human Motivation."[3] The paper postulated that human behavior is driven by our unrelenting efforts to fulfill five categories of essential human needs: physiological, safety, love and belonging, esteem, and self-actualization. Utilizing a five-tiered pyramid (see Figure 4.2), Maslow argued that the satisfaction of each need is reliant upon the fulfillment of the ones that are more foundational. For Maslow, this meant that achieving self-actualization is a relative rarity because—due to societal pressures and influences—individuals must exert constant energy to fulfill the basic and psychological needs required in order to create the capacity to self-actualize.

In other words, if you don't have your most basic physiological needs—air, water, shelter, food, sleep—fulfilled, higher-level development is nearly impossible. "A Theory of Human Motivation" was written more than eighty years ago, but Maslow's work endures. His model can help us identify the gaps in our own individual needs pyramid and then consider how we might fill them so we can overcome the obstacles they create. In doing this, we

Figure 4.2. Maslow's Hierarchy

can set the stage for unlimited personal development. Let's examine the hierarchy one level at a time.

Physiological Needs

Maslow believed that the lowest levels of needs had to be satisfied before the upper levels could be achieved (Figure 4.2). If you are starving, you are not worried about your self-esteem. No matter what privileges or disadvantages an individual has, if they experience *true hunger*—not just the sensation of being hungry but rather deprivation of essential nutrition—their higher-level sense of equity and justice will not be activated. A starving person focuses solely on obtaining food. They think about it, dream about it, and seek it out at all costs. As you can imagine, someone who lacks their basic needs has very adverse initial conditions.

In America today, physiological needs are not always met, despite well-intentioned government programs, local charities, and food banks. According to nokidhungry.org, thirty-seven million (11.4 percent of all Americans) live in poverty.[4] That group includes twelve million children. It should incense us that a country of such immense wealth and opportunity still has this problem to solve.

Imagine a society in which the physiological needs of all people, including children, were met. It would be a defining human achievement, enabling the evolution of a culture marked by greater social cohesion, improved mental health, and expanded intellectual and creative capabilities. The effect would be exponential in a society in which all physiological needs were met.

Safety Needs

The second level of Maslow's hierarchy is safety needs. These encompass the desire for physical safety, security, stability, and protection. This is probably more relevant to many of us because we have all encountered situations where we did not feel physically safe, whether it be bullying at school, an angry parent, conflict in a neighborhood, or in a particularly dangerous location and circumstance.

Here are some sobering statistics on bullying in the United States from the National Center for Education Statistics (2021–22).

- Around 19 percent of students ages twelve to eighteen report being bullied at school.
- Nearly 30 percent of students in the United States report being bullied online.
- In a recent study, about one in five students reported being bullied at some point in their lives.
- About 64 percent of children who were bullied did not report the incident to an adult.
- Boys are more likely to experience physical bullying, while girls are more likely to experience verbal and social bullying.[5]

The desire to feel secure in your surroundings—physical safety—is common to us all. Consider where your children live or go to school. Do they feel safe? Existing in a dangerous situation makes essential growth—let alone true emergence—impossible. Without a basic level of physical safety, children may experience heightened levels of anxiety, fear, and stress, which can impact their overall well-being and inhibit their ability to thrive. In this situation, children struggle to progress.

This is very much linked to the need for emotional stability, which has become a struggle for many of us in the modern age. With the impact of increased anxiety due to the never-ending rat race, ever-present social media, and a general lack of empathy, the sense of security that was once an inherent aspect of our families and schools has been diminished.

Another critical component of our safety needs is stability. This includes having a sense of predictability and certainty in one's life, such as financial resources, school, or family to rely on. This is a reminder of the balance we need to strike between chaos and order. If you live with a high level of chaos, it will work directly against your child's progress.

This level also includes financial stability, which is essential for meeting basic needs like food, shelter, and healthcare. Without a stable source of income, individuals feel vulnerable, not knowing where their next meal will come from.

We will end with a piece of advice from my late father, Paul J. Strecker. To this day, I believe his wise words: "Money can't buy happiness, but a lack of it sure can make things difficult."

Love and Belonging

Human beings, especially children, are social by nature, and the need for love and belonging is essential for their emotional well-being. We all crave social connections and intimacy, but going without them when you are young and vulnerable changes the brain for the worse.

A sense of belonging can come from various sources such as family, friends, schools, faith-based or social organizations, and even our geographic communities. Without these connections, one may feel isolated and lonely, leading to negative emotional health.

Do you recall your earliest school days? Did they provide you with love and belonging?

I still remember my first day of kindergarten walking into the front door of Shumaker Elementary School. I was full from my breakfast. Feeling safe, I walked right in as the teacher ushered me into the classroom. My first instinct was to look around for companionship. Even at our youngest, we are programmed to look for friendship. Being accepted is engrained in us. It didn't take me long, and I partnered up with a child named Bob. He remains my best friend to this day. I am also friends on Facebook with many of my elementary school friends. Special thank you to Mrs. Redd and Mrs. Sarty, who, as teachers, nurtured a sense of love and belonging for all the children in their classrooms.

One important realm of the love and belonging tier that I feel we must address for our older students and children is modern dating. I believe we have taken a step back as we have implemented convenience techniques. Building meaningful pair-bonding relationships has become more complicated in today's fast-paced, technology-driven world. Social media platforms have made it easier to connect with others. However, they also contribute to feelings of loneliness if relationships are fostered virtually. Developing strong bonds with others can improve well-being, social skill building, and physical health; however, today's virtual dating techniques have made relationship-seeking much more complicated.

Let's look at an example as the world has become more connected, but superficially so. As my son got older, he asked me for dating advice. Here is what I advised.

- Be confident and kind. When asking a girl out, be polite and specific about where you would like to take her on the date. I recommend a nice dinner date where you can take time to get to know each other. Offer to pay, but if she wants to split the bill, you should agree.
- Be chivalrous. Open doors, show good manners, and respect and honor her.
- Be a good listener.
- Never try to kiss her on the first date. You need to take time to develop a healthy relationship.

After a few attempts, he replied, "Dad, I have tried all your techniques, but that is no longer how the world works."

After scoffing at him, I began to research modern dating. Oh, how times have changed. Here is the "new and improved system," I say with skepticism and through a lens of complexity.

- Online dating creates a shallow atmosphere of connection. How much can you get to know a person from an online profile? In days past, you would often become friends before dating, but that is less the case in this new virtual matchmaking world. Quantity has been prioritized over quality.
- Effect on Young Men: The abundance of options has also created a hyper-competitive dating marketplace, with the top 10 percent of men receiving 80 percent of the positive responses from females. With that kind of unbalanced response set, those men are not looking to find Mrs. Right but Ms. Right-Now. When I was younger, these men were called "players," but all the girls knew who they were due to localized dating. Now, there is no way of knowing, because online dating removes the personal side of reputation building. I'm sad to say that for the other 90 percent of men, many are lost in this virtual world.
- Effect on Young Women: Without a personal connection and most women dating a small group of men, "ghosting" (suddenly ceasing all communication without explanation) has become prevalent. The accountability side of interactions seems to be removed from the dating process. Men no longer give females the courtesy of saying, "This isn't working," to their faces. They just disappear. This makes it harder for women to form meaningful relationships and develop trust in men. As a result, you often hear, "Where have all the good men gone?"

Not only is this new style of dating tricky for both boys and girls of all sexual orientations, but it also works directly against developing a strong sense of love and belonging. Meaningful human interaction requires commitment, trust, effort, and respect. But putting in this extra effort feels too strenuous in today's world built for our convenience.

It is a good thing we are not forced to choose our schools, friendships, families, and communities by swiping left or right. Well, not yet anyway. By nurturing positive relationships and building a supportive network of people around you, you create a sense of belonging that enhances your emotional resilience. This can even include the city or town in which you live.

I currently live in a small town called Ligonier, Pennsylvania. Ligonier has a bustling vibrancy to it, emanating love and belonging. The residents celebrate Fort Days, Ice Sculpture Days, Christmas Light Up Nights, and many more bonding occasions. Residents feel safe, wanted, and welcome. After eight years here, I am still committed to participating actively in this beautiful community.

I encourage you and your children to get involved in your school, town, or neighborhood in order to find and cultivate belonging. You will be able to make a substantial difference to others with your newly developed skills. You may wonder how much one person can accomplish. The power of belonging and competence produces the likes of Gandhi, Mother Teresa, and Dr. Martin Luther King Jr. One may not reach worldwide fame, but they might be that beloved person in their school or local community.

Ultimately, achieving love and belonging is essential for personal growth and self-actualization, according to Maslow's theory. When you feel connected and loved by others, you are better equipped to pursue your full potential and goals. You can create a strong foundation for self-fulfillment and happiness by prioritizing healthy relationships and nurturing social connections.

Esteem Needs

Maslow identifies esteem needs as the fourth level of motivation. This level addresses internal needs such as self-confidence, self-respect, and a positive self-image. Also, it addresses external esteem needs, such as recognition and prestige. Fulfilling these needs is crucial for developing a sense of achievement.

To satisfy esteem needs, children often seek validation and approval from others. This can come in the form of praise and respect from your peers or society. Conversely, a lack of positive feedback (or constant criticism) can lead to feelings of inadequacy. However, cultivating a healthy sense of self-worth allows a child to recognize their strengths and capabilities, regardless of external validation.

Consider the children you support. Are you kind? Have they developed a high level of trust with you? Are you transparent and honest in a supportive way?

A funny thing can happen when you develop high levels of trust with another person. I once had a boss I greatly admired, Mr. Maher, the Head of School at the John Cooper School in Texas, where I was the Middle School Division Head. He would make humorous statements in times of heightened stress. I learned it was his way of showing admiration and respect.

It was late May and I was getting ready to conduct our eighth-grade graduation ceremony. I was responsible for ensuring the event was run successfully. The Performing Arts Center was filled to capacity, and I was a bit nervous. I was standing just offstage. Mr. Maher walked up, leaned in, and whispered, "Hey, Jon, big crowd today, don't screw this up." He smiled and walked off to take his seat. I started to laugh. I knew Mr. Maher was attempting to calm me down and wishing me luck. Early on in our relationship, he would often come up quietly in profound moments and tell me, "Jon, you did a great job today." That built my confidence. After developing a deep bond over the years, I developed a strong sense of self-worth, and his teasing became affectionate and comical to me. Thank you, Mike.

Maslow also recognizes the need for autonomy in our esteem needs. The only way for someone to earn true self-confidence and self-respect is for them to experience the necessary freedom to earn their own accolades. If too much control is exerted upon a person, as we discussed in Chapter 3, that person will never feel fully accomplished.

My mom used to leave us a honey-do list on the weekends: wash dishes, bring down laundry, make the bed, etc. We called it the *yellow mom list of torture* on account of the yellow-lined paper she often used. Have you ever been given a similar list? When a person leaves a list, I find it disheartening as it does not allow me to feel good about completing the requisite tasks. However, one day, instead of leaving me a list, my mom asked if I could help get the house in order. This extra autonomy encouraged me to clean the entire house. I did ten times the work and enjoyed every moment. In the end, autonomy leads to motivation, motivation to accomplishment, and accomplishment to esteem.

Teachers understand this concept. Your children likely receive stickers from teachers at your school, and your child likely shows them to you when they get home. A common practice is that you then show pride by hanging these symbols of accomplishment on the refrigerator. This validation is a good start at helping your child develop positive self-esteem. However, as children grow up, a subtle shift should occur away from parents expressing *their* pride for their child to encouraging the child to feel proud *of themselves*. A simple, "You should be proud of yourself" goes a long way in transitioning the focus from external to internal validation. This small, yet significant change reinforces a child's autonomy and self-esteem.

Developing a positive self-image and a strong sense of self-worth requires self-awareness, self-acceptance, and self-confidence. The operative word is *self*. This internal sense of esteem is essential for navigating life's challenges and pursuing personal growth and fulfillment. We cannot solely rely on others for approval.

Society, however, has fallen prey to the philosophy of false praise. We often congratulate people for mediocre efforts to boost their confidence. Many people give praise so readily, in fact, that the children question its authenticity. Since self-confidence is obtained internally, not given, we must be truthful, even when the truth may be less than glowing. We do not want to hurt anyone intentionally. However, by being consistently authentic, we ensure that children who receive our praise will be certain of its credibility. As a practice, we should focus on complimenting the child's effort rather than the outcome. This leaves room for improvement and prioritizes growth over results. Let's use an example:

Let's say you have a student produce a draft document for the school newspaper. For the first time, you have given them the autonomy to create a rough draft independently. The goal lies in increasing self-confidence and moving them toward independence. Ultimately, you want them to produce these types of documents on their own with competence.

They hand over the document when finished. You can tell it has taken them extensive time, but it needs to be up to expectations, which it is not. You can handle the situation in a few ways.

1. Tell them they've done great work and make the needed edits. However, they see all your edits when the article is released. Their self-confidence will be diminished.
2. Sit down with them and go over the document step by step. On occasion, you need to assert this level of control to ensure excellence, especially if there is a deadline. However, doing this too frequently can cause stagnation.
3. Tell them you appreciate all the hard work (validation), provide feedback, and ask them to go back to the document and improve it. They go back to the document and continue to struggle. They improve their skills, ultimately producing the desired results. The adversity leads to skill development, autonomy, and confidence. Like a self-reinforcing system, as confidence grows, so does productivity, joy for the job, the desire to improve, and collegiality. They know your praise is authentic. Internal validation is accomplished. And you are able to rely on their skills here forward. Win-win.

Self-Actualization

Self-actualization represents the highest level in Maslow's hierarchy of needs. It is a state of personal fulfillment and creativity characterized by a deep sense of purpose and meaning. During the self-actualizing stage, a person becomes the best version of themselves. According to Maslow, the process involves pursuing one's passions and values—executing one's vision. For us as schools and parents, this takes a lifetime of work so it will not be accomplished within their childhood years. However, if you remember back to our fractal structuring, our work can help provide them with the foundation needed to reach actualization.

An inner desire for self-improvement and personal development drives self-actualized individuals. We can reinforce in children the need to constantly seek new challenges, set ambitious goals, and push themselves beyond their comfort zones. This pursuit of growth and self-discovery is a lifelong journey. It involves embracing change, learning from failures, and striving for exceptionalism. It is a complex journey, but with effort, greatness can emerge in those you influence.

Maslow believed that self-actualization is rare and attainable for only a tiny percentage of individuals who have fulfilled the hierarchy's other levels of needs. However, he also believed that everyone, including you as the teacher and parent, has the potential to achieve self-actualization by embracing personal growth. By recognizing and nurturing your strengths, core values, and purpose, you can approach a meaningful and fulfilling existence and share it with those fortunate children you help motivate.

Those who reach this stage will have satisfied all of their needs and overcome the constraints of their initial conditions. This is an incredibly privileged position to be in. However, this privilege is born out of a commitment to exceptionalism rather than circumstance. If you reach this level yourself, never pretend it was simple, for we all know self-actualized individuals seek a complex and strenuous path.

For me, self-actualization is represented in the authoring of this book. I have been thinking about writing it for more than fifteen years. While I am only now putting my fingers to the keyboard, my entire life has been spent trying to understand the holistic nature of human development. Along the way, I have learned from many incredible thinkers.

SUMMARY

- Initial conditions—including both privileges and disadvantages—exist for all of us.
- Maslow's Hierarchy explains the five levels of human needs in priority order. They enable us to determine what we have and what we are lacking, so we can find solutions to fulfill our unmet needs. These solutions might very well produce meaningful results as we try to minimize disparities in society based on socioeconomic status, race, religion, gender, etc.
- Our physiological needs are our most basic requirements for survival such as food, water, and air to breathe.
- Our safety needs include protection, stability, and security.
- Our need for love and belonging includes friendship, family, community, and intimacy.
- Our esteem needs include self-confidence, respect, and acknowledgment.
- Self-actualization means becoming our best self by fulfilling our vision for our future.

PART II

ACHIEVING EMERGENCE: THE FIVE INTELLIGENCES

In Chapters 5–9, I will discuss the five fundamental attributes of success: physical, intellectual, social, emotional, and ethical intelligence. Although these areas of development will be presented separately, you will quickly notice the overlap and connection among them. Additionally, in Chapter 10, I will emphasize how these five key attributes are self-reinforcing.

I have selected Bloom's Taxonomy as a framework to explore each developmental area and its applications. You will progress from curiosity to wisdom as you examine each level. This practice aims to encourage you to apply the taxonomy to any area you wish to understand more thoroughly.

CHAPTER FIVE

DEVELOPING PHYSICAL INTELLIGENCE

*Physical strength is the most important thing in life.
This is true whether we want it to be or not.*
—MARK RIPPETOE[1]

We often take our physical health for granted, especially in children. As schools reduce recess, gym classes, and outdoor class time, children have less and less time to move their bodies. This is all in an effort to ensure intellectual benchmarks. We forgot, as educational professionals, that physical health is an essential element to cognitive success. The two elements are inextricably linked.

This situation has been magnified at home, as parents have become increasingly cautious about allowing their children to play outside unsupervised. Parents have been conditioned to consider every unknown person, place, and thing as a potential threat. As a result, parents defend their children as a mother bear would defend her cubs. Compounding this issue is the abundance of technology that competes with children's natural curiosity and desire for physical outdoor play. The allure of the virtual world is dynamic for the child, and from the parent's perspective, safe. Ironically, the virtual world holds countless dangers, such as child predators and social bullying, using the anonymity of the space as a personal hunting ground. As a result, the decline in physical health among children has reached epidemic proportions. When physical health is compromised, nothing else truly matters.

I can speak with firsthand knowledge.

A WAKE-UP CALL

I want to share a personal experience as a cautionary tale. In 1991, after my first few quarters at The Ohio State University, I went to work at Cedar Point Amusement Park in Sandusky, Ohio for the summer. For the previous six months, I had been struggling with some unusual symptoms: night sweats, vision loss, weight loss, and fatigue. As a result, I made an appointment with my family doctor.

After a few tests, I vividly remember sitting in his office, waiting for him to return with my results. I instinctually knew something was wrong, as the nurses moved in and out nervously, and there was a palpable sense of dread. Finally, the lead nurse asked me to call my parents. I wasn't sure why, but I called my mom and dad, asking them to come to the hospital.

Before my parents could arrive, the doctor entered the room and sat across from me. I had known him all my life. When he looked up at me, I noticed his eyes filled with tears. I could tell he didn't want to deliver the news. Just then, my mother and father walked in.

"Jon, it appears you have cancer. It is pretty far along and we have to make some difficult decisions pretty quickly. The cancer is next to your lungs, but I do not know exactly where it has moved to."

After undergoing a biopsy, numerous blood tests, and a visit to a reproductive center, I learned that I had stage IV Hodgkin's disease, which led to the start of my chemotherapy treatment. I spent the next year fighting for my life, enduring seven months of chemotherapy followed by three months of radiation. Thanks to the compassion and care of Dr. Thornton and the James Cancer Hospital at Ohio State, I entered remission.

The cancer and its treatment changed my life forever. Chemotherapy had a negative impact on all my organs, and the radiation affected my heart and lungs. I survived. However, I've been engaged in a constant health battle since I was twenty-one years old. Given the circumstances, I consider myself blessed and conditionally healthy.

Things were mostly stable until 2017. I had just begun my new position as Head of School and was excited for the start of the school year at Valley School of Ligonier. However, in late September, I began to experience unusual symptoms again. I remember feeling chills, shortness of breath, pain in my left arm, and extreme fatigue. Since my heart had always been damaged, I was somewhat accustomed to these symptoms. However, when they reached a level of intensity I had never experienced before, I decided to schedule a doctor's appointment for the following week.

That evening, though, I felt terrible. My wife could see how I was struggling. Not willing to take any chances, she insisted, "Let's go, right now." We arrived at the emergency room entrance twenty minutes later. I hopped out of the car and walked in on my own. Within five minutes, I was hooked up to an ECG with an IV in my arm, and everyone around me looked nervous.

After a flurry of activity, I remember looking at the nurse and saying, "I don't feel well," and then my vision narrowed. She said, "Take a deep breath."

A few minutes later, I woke up to the doctor tapping my cheek, "Mr. Strecker, Mr. Strecker." Thinking I fainted and trying to be funny, I squeaked out, "Doctor Strecker."

I could tell by the look on the doctor's face that he was not amused.

It wasn't until after I had been stabilized that I learned I had gone into cardiac arrest and they had to shock my heart back into rhythm. I needed to be transferred to a larger hospital with more facilities. The UPMC staff in Pittsburgh got me up into the operating room quickly; Dr. Lee cleared the blockage in the "widow maker" artery and put in a few stents.

Since then, I have learned to embrace the chaos and order of my situation. My body is constantly fighting to move me toward disorder, but my doctors and I try to apply the right amount of control to keep me stabilized. This is a challenging reality that many of us face, as I am not alone in battling for my health on a daily basis.

I understand that this is an extreme example of health challenges, but it has helped me recognize the importance of appreciating a healthy lifestyle. While my cancer was unavoidable, I have come to realize that many health issues children face today can be prevented.

A CRISIS IN HEALTH

Here are some statistics from the World Health Organization:

- In 2022, one in eight individuals worldwide grappled with obesity.
- Adult obesity has more than doubled globally since 1990, while adolescent obesity has quadrupled.

- In 2022, 2.5 billion adults (aged eighteen and above) were overweight, with 890 million classified as obese.
- 43 percent of adults aged eighteen and above were overweight in 2022, and 16 percent were classified as obese.
- In 2022, 37 million children under the age of five were overweight.
- Over 390 million children and adolescents aged five to nineteen years were overweight in 2022, with 160 million classified as obese.[2]

These are alarming trends. As educational professionals and parents, we must reassess our practices and proactively address these problems before it's too late.

Instead, in the modern day, we have been conditioned to focus on solutions that reject the physical dangers for emotional and social reasons.

An example of this is body positivity.

First, I will begin with the benefits of body positivity. In its authentic form, it advocates that people of all shapes and sizes deserve love and belonging, should feel positive about themselves, and should develop a healthy relationship with food. Indeed, advocating for this approach is appropriate, since one's physical health does not define or connote one's intelligence, mental health, social skills, or moral capabilities. Obesity, for instance, does not mean a person (myself included, currently more than three hundred pounds as I type this sentence) is incapable of becoming self-actualized.

However, let me also explain why this movement has become twisted by some to encourage a dangerous perspective on health. If obesity is ignored entirely, in the name of body positivity, it can cause terrible outcomes. It increases the likelihood of cardiovascular disease, sleep apnea, cancer, and respiratory issues, and it reduces life expectancy. Make no mistake about it. We cannot dismiss the reality that comes with unhealthy living, especially in our children.

Let me use an analogy. If a child has dyslexia, we don't pretend that the condition doesn't exist or that we should simply encourage them with positive thoughts while ignoring the issue. Instead, we identify the problem and provide the necessary support through a tailored learning plan, allowing the child to thrive intellectually while building the child up emotionally. We should do the same with physical health.

THE PHYSICAL HEALTH DAMAGE DONE BY EDUCATIONAL DECISION-MAKING, MEDIA MANIPULATION, AND VIRTUAL EXISTENCE

As we reflect on the choices made in education and the advent of modern conveniences, particularly the impact of a virtual existence, it becomes evident that our collective physical health has declined. This deterioration is largely a result of the negative consequences associated with our increasingly sedentary lifestyles.

Let's go back in time a bit. As a child in the 1980s, our distractions were limited. We had fewer than ten channels on the television, mostly fuzzy and out of focus. The Atari 2600 was one of the more prominent gaming systems. Needless to say, those 8-bit graphics did not keep our attention. The news came on twice a day for thirty to sixty minutes per broadcast, and none of the highly addictive social media sites existed. As a result, many of the conveniences that exist today were either in their infancy or nonexistent. I mean, even the mobile telephones were the size of bricks.

The benefit of this was that our lives were filled with imagination and physical discovery. During long days, we played sports, ran through sprinklers, and swam in the local pool. During the evening, we played Ghost in the Graveyard, flashlight tag, and basketball under the yellow glow of the streetlights. Our neighbors were our friends and helped guard against physical harm.

So, what has happened to these fun-loving times? You have to look no further than the impact of three critical areas (educational reform, sensationalized news media, and the distraction of virtual existence).

Educational Reform

In the 2000s, as the effects of the No Child Left Behind Act solidified, education began to separate the areas of development into their constituent parts. Instead of aiming to help children grow holistically (intellectually, socially, emotionally, ethically, and physically), schools made short-sighted decisions like *less recess and more math*. On the surface, it made sense, but my oh my, what a simplistic error. Physical education and recess were the first things to be reduced or cut from school curricula.

What has this decision wrought? Not only have the academic struggles grown worse, but we have made the physical health issues more prominent, along with social, emotional, and ethical declines. But we will get to that later.

In the three schools where I have worked, all of them have ensured that students in grades K–8 have daily recess, gym, or athletics. I have observed that, in many cases, our eighth graders enjoy as much or even more recess time than many public school lower-grade students. I want to clarify that I am not criticizing the teachers in these schools; rather, I am highlighting a bureaucracy that undervalues physical health as part of a comprehensive educational approach.

Sensationalized News Media

To fill the twenty-four-hour news cycle and attract dedicated viewers, the media have sensationalized both local and global events. This exaggerated awareness has led parents to perceive dangers that are often minimal or nonexistent. Consequently, children and parents now adopt a defensive mindset fueled by irrational fear rather than a mindset of childhood discovery. Added to this, neighbors no longer support one another; instead, families' heightened fears cause them to view neighbors as potential threats.

As a result, young children today are confined to their homes, and healthy physical play outside has been diminished.

Virtual Existence

Social media has exacerbated children's sedentary lifestyles, disrupted their sleep, increased their anxiety, and negatively affected their eating habits. On top of this detrimental cocktail, addictive attributes embedded into the technology by developers create a desire loop that keeps them hooked and constantly clamoring for more.

As if children weren't already vulnerable enough, we are now on the verge of creating an experience that could be even more enticing and damaging to their lives—virtual AI. Unfortunately, this new reality is being celebrated as something we must simply accept. I refuse to accept it. I want you to take a moment and imagine this world.

After a long day of navigating the real world at school, your eighth-grade son arrives home from school. He heads to his room and says, "I just want to unwind for a bit." He slips on a fitted haptic suit and immersive goggles equipped with the best noise-cancelation technology available and enters a world of unimaginable bliss. Thanks to advanced AI technology, the suit creates an endless array of scenarios tailored for a young man of his age. Without having to move a muscle, he scores the winning touchdown in the championship game, becomes the most popular boy in school, asks out the prettiest girl to the dance (who, of course, says yes as programmed), and radiates confidence.

You might say, "Wow, that sounds like a wonderful experience." However, if we take a step back, this allows an impressionable young man to experience well beyond just physical greatness without having developed the necessary skills to achieve it in reality.

Let me ask a question: Do you think a young person would rather exist in an adversity-filled reality or in the perpetual bliss of this virtual world? It should certainly give us pause.

THE BRAIN-BODY CONNECTION: PROTECTING COGNITIVE FUNCTION AND WELL-BEING

Hopefully, these warnings have captured your attention.

Let's delve a little deeper into why it's so important to nurture a child's physical health. While the importance of fitness for overall well-being has been long studied and widely acknowledged, its direct impact on brain function and the intricate relationship between mind and body has garnered more attention recently. We must understand and appreciate that, if children ignore their physical health, they hinder their other intelligences.

Let me explain. The human brain is the body's control center; it's responsible for processing information, regulating emotions, and coordinating bodily functions. It is the most complex organ in our body, a symphony of electrical and chemical signals adapted to ensure peak performance. A child's body's job is to guarantee the brain receives the sustenance it needs to work optimally. Their bodies' vitality depends on three components, *the Big Three—adequate nutrition, regular exercise, and restorative sleep*. When considering your child, you must ask the following questions: Are they eating right, getting enough sleep, and working out regularly to ensure their brain processes information at peak performance?

Let's consider real-world impacts.

IMPACTS

Oxygen and Nutrient Supply: The brain is a metabolically active organ, meaning it requires a constant supply of oxygen and nutrients to function efficiently. With cardiovascular exercise, a child ensures the supply of these by enhancing blood circulation. Moreover, a balanced diet rich in vitamins, minerals, and antioxidants supports brain health, facilitating neurotransmitter synthesis and cellular repair.

Before my cardiac arrest incident in 2017, I was not receiving enough oxygen or nutrients to my brain. I didn't realize I was oxygen and nutrient insufficient at the time, but my symptoms were striking, including impaired memory, blurred vision, processing issues, and a speech impediment. I wasn't sure what was happening then, but in retrospect, I can assure you a brain deprived of oxygen and nutrients does not function well.

Eating well and deep breathing exercises are a great way to ensure the brain is fully fueled.

Stress Reduction: Chronic stress has harmful effects on brain function. It impairs cognitive performance and increases the risk of mental health disorders. Physical activity acts as a natural stress reliever and reduces cortisol levels, the primary stress hormone.

After my cardiac arrest incident, I developed post-traumatic stress disorder (PTSD). I couldn't stop thinking about that event and how mere seconds separated me from life and death. The symptoms I experienced made it difficult for me to process information correctly. I responded to every little physical twinge or uncomfortable feeling with a sense of dread and panic. Eventually, I spoke to my brother, who had a similar experience after his time in the Marines. He gave me valuable advice: to talk to my doctor and seek professional help. One of the greatest benefits of my recovery was taking peaceful walks in the woods, disconnected from technology. These walks provided me with the physical activity I needed, along with the peace and tranquility that helped me heal.

What strategies does your child use to decompress from their busy lives? I recommend attuning your child to the healing powers of nature, reading books, and meditation, separate from the allure of the frantic pace of a technologically driven world.

Sleep Quality: As much as a child's physical health improves by playing for fun, their brain health improves when they go to sleep. Quality sleep is essential for brain health, facilitating memory consolidation, synaptic pruning, and neurotoxin clearance. Regular exercise improves sleep quality by regulating circadian rhythms and promoting more profound, restorative sleep.

I mentioned that I struggled as a young learner, and one of the reasons for this was likely my lack of quality sleep. I frequently experienced nightmares that led to sleepless nights. I would regularly wake at 3:33 a.m. after vivid nightmares. I'm still not sure why I awakened with such consistency, but these restless nights often left my mind fragmented the next day, causing my attention to shift between clarity and clouded thoughts.

Monitoring your child's sleep is one of the more underutilized skills we consider as parents. I recommend asking your child how restfully they slept. You can ask, how many times do you think you awoke during the night? Did you have nice dreams? Do you feel rested? These are clues to the essential elements of a peaceful night of rest.

The connection between body health and brain function is undeniable. By prioritizing physical fitness, nutrition, and sleep, we can optimize a child's cognitive performance and mental well-being. Prioritizing body health in support of brain function is essential for fostering lifelong cognitive vitality.

SMALL STEPS TOWARD A POSITIVE TIPPING POINT

Creating a lifelong plan for physical health can be challenging. Much of the literature on this topic presents quick and simplistic strategies, such as crash diets and overly ambitious workout routines. Instead of focusing on how to address our unhealthy behaviors in the long term, we often seek short-term fixes that usually lead to temporary results. To achieve lasting health, we should develop a more complex and holistic approach, similar to how we cultivate our intellectual growth.

If complexity teaches us anything, it's that we must look at the multiple factors that go into a healthy lifestyle. Let's begin with an example from a personal friend.

Tommy Mygrant has had one of the most dramatic physical fitness transformations I have ever witnessed. P90X—Beachbody Fitness recognized him as a man of exceptional commitment. When I think about Tommy's ability to apply force (his relentless effort) to a chaotic system (his lifelong physical habits), I am inspired to use his story as an illustration of how one achieves exceptionalism to overcome obstacles.

As a young adult, Tommy was an intelligent, friendly, confident, honest young man who was a bit heavy. By his early thirties, Tommy had fallen into a rut, as many of us do. As the days turned into weeks, and the weeks into years, he spent his days selling insurance and his nights playing online poker. As there was very little time committed to exercise and he didn't consider his diet, his health suffered. In many ways, he was living an unfulfilled life without any sense of direction or purpose. One day, he found himself at his doctor's office. His doctor told him that it was time to put him on medications to control his cholesterol and blood pressure, and likely for the rest of his life.

Many of us in this situation might have resigned ourselves to accepting this fate. Maybe you are accepting your life as it is right now. But we all have a choice.

A feeling welled up inside Tommy in that moment. He understood his body was becoming entropic. Chaos was taking over, and his body was reacting negatively to his obesity. Would he resign himself to his fate or do something he had never done before? He suddenly saw an opportunity to do the unthinkable. This was a tipping point.

Tommy realized that this would be a difficult journey with no easy steps. He would need to muster a tremendous amount of physical and mental effort to change his body and, by extension, his life. One of the benefits of the P90X program is that it is designed to make substantial changes incrementally. As such, Tommy began to change his life one tiny step at a time. Through fractal growth he developed a foundation of gradual improvement.

Tommy talks about his early days on the program and his inability to mirror what the workout hosts did in their videos. He had to keep a positive mindset throughout to persevere: "It's OK to modify. It's OK not to keep up with the guys in the video. The first time, I couldn't do 20 percent of what they were doing."

Undeterred, Tommy kept working toward his goal of becoming healthy by achieving micro improvements. Gradually, something deep inside him

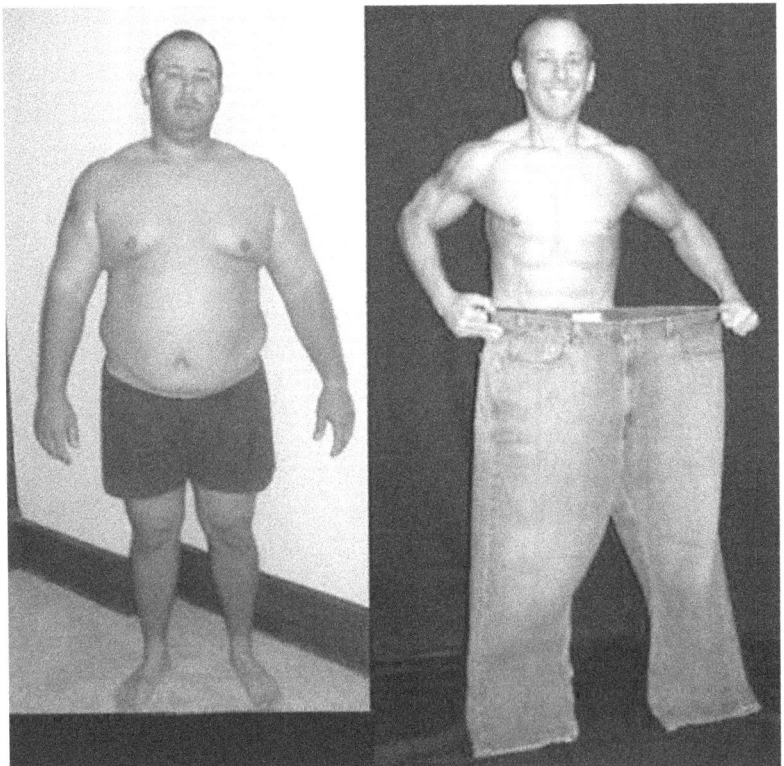

Figure 5.1. Tommy Mygrant

changed. He became motivated beyond basic health to the point of true physical exceptionalism. His miniature triumphs grew to enormous proportions over the course of a year and a half. Keep in mind, the program is hard to do for ninety days. For Tommy to reach his goal took 450 days (see Figure 5.1).

Regardless of the chaos in his life, his genetics, and his past lifestyle, Tommy applied the right amount of effort over enough time, with the correct level of control and autonomy to achieve the remarkable. He placed himself in a box (Box System in Chapter 3) and pressed down hard upon it with enough intensity to become extraordinary.

We should appreciate those who, like Tommy, achieve the unimaginable. These are the people who become the true difference-makers. These are the types of success stories we must pass along to our children when they are young, so they begin their lives with the right habits in mind.

THE POWER OF THE EXTRA DEGREE

I often present to my students at Valley School the importance of a *tipping point*. Sustained effort is not always recognizable when we begin to apply it. Sometimes you may not feel or see the results immediately, but when you do—wow! It can make all the difference.

In the book *212° The Extra Degree*, Sam Parker uses the idea of heating water as a metaphor.[3] As we put water in a pot, turn on the stove, and begin to heat it, there is little noticeable effect as the water warms. Force is being applied to the water, but the desired results might not be obvious to the observer. You may have experienced something similar as your child has worked toward a goal.

Have you experienced watching a child put in a substantial effort trying to better themselves, but after some time, without any noticeable results, they decide the method isn't working? Disappointed, some give up. That is simple thinking. Complex thinkers know to wait, looking for minute levels of progress. Those micro improvements are hard to see as a child patiently persists. Yet, once that tipping point is reached, watch out.

At water's tipping point, it changes from a liquid to a gas. With this gas, we can push forward a locomotive or a steamship, or generate power in nuclear reactors. Similarly, the efforts may not seem to be having an impact, but with continued exertion, that hard work will manifest with a level of exceptionalism as it did with my friend Tommy.

APPLYING BLOOM'S TAXONOMY TO PHYSICAL DEVELOPMENT

I chose to start with physical health when describing the five intelligences because it's easiest to physically recognize one's progress. A person can literally see and feel the improvements they are making, even if it takes time. When one strategically analyzes one's physical health, using Bloom's Taxonomy (see Figure 5.2), one will be able to recognize how each level promotes a healthy brain and body. Let's start with what you need to know.

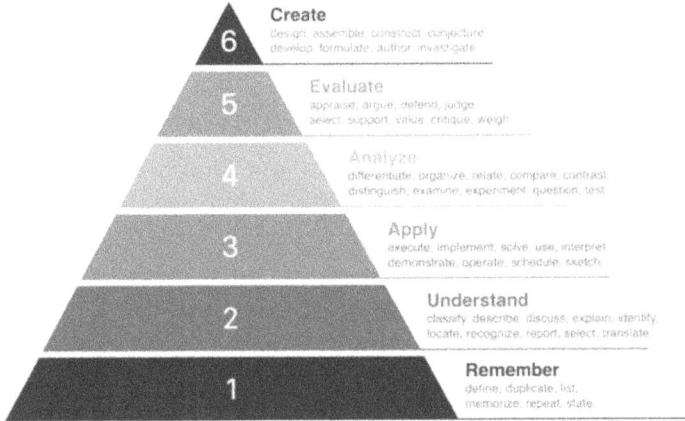
Figure 5.2. Bloom's Taxonomy (Revised 2001)

REMEMBER

It's worth committing a certain level of information about physical development to memory so that it's readily accessible and can inform a child's daily habits and behaviors. Here are a few essential notes that will inform your child's journey toward good health:

- A child's cells specialize in specific tasks and need nutrients and water to function well. This is provided through the blood.
- Bones provide the structure and protection for the body.
- Muscles power the internal operating system (think moving, breathing, and beating heart).
- The skin protects, heals, and regulates body temperature.
- The brain is the command center; the information pathway is the spinal cord.
- Genes carry your genetic code, differentiating us from one another in terms of hair color, eye color, height, skin color, and everything else.

UNDERSTAND

Take care of your body. It is the only place you have to live.
—JIM ROHN[4]

A healthy body encompasses a multifaceted perspective beyond mere physical appearance. Here are several vital aspects to consider:

- **Lifestyle Choices:** A healthy body is a result of conscious lifestyle choices. This includes engaging in regular physical activity, consuming a balanced diet rich in nutrients, getting adequate sleep, and avoiding harmful habits such as smoking and excessive alcohol consumption. Remember, we are role models for our children, and our actions speak louder than words. Be mindful of your lifestyle choices.
- **Preventive Health:** Prioritizing a healthy body involves preventive measures to avoid illness. These include scheduling regular check-ups with healthcare professionals, including your child's eyes, teeth, and ears.

The process is not always pleasant. I just got back from stuffing my six-foot-six-inch, three-hundred-plus-pound body into an MRI machine for forty-five minutes to check a spot on my pancreas. I felt like a sausage packed into its casing. When the test was complete, I felt mentally and physically better knowing the truth of what was happening; it lowered my stress, reminded me of the preciousness of life, and gave my family peace—a small price to pay for the temporary pain. Your children might push back on the doctor or dentist, but knowing is better for long-term health than short-term discomfort.

- **Physical Fitness:** Physical fitness is a critical component of a healthy body. This includes cardiovascular endurance, muscular strength, flexibility, and a healthy body composition. Engaging in different types of physical activities, such as aerobic exercises and strength training, helps maintain overall fitness levels.
- **Nutrition:** Proper nutrition is essential for supporting bodily functions, maintaining energy levels, and preventing nutrient deficiencies. A balanced diet of fruits, vegetables, whole grains, lean proteins, and healthy fats provides essential nutrients for optimal health.

I am known at my school as a dessert junkie. I regularly conduct surprise "inspections" of the kitchen hoping I can grab a mini pack of Oreos (containing two of those devilishly delicious treats). However, since we are committed to healthy nutrition at our school, the chefs at Valley School instead offer up a bag of carrots. When this happens, my taste buds may depart disappointed, but my mind knows the carrots will nourish me better than cookies, and I feel grateful for the people in my life who care about my best interests—another reminder of the importance of keeping good company.

> **Mind-Body Connection:** Recognizing the interconnectedness of the mind and body is crucial for overall well-being. Mindfulness and relaxation can help promote harmony in both.

Mental health issues can manifest physically, such as attention deficit hyperactivity disorder (ADHD). In recent years, we have seen a spike in diagnoses. However, although it's traditionally seen as a physical affliction caused by genetics, neuroscientists have recently recognized that excessive screen time can cause symptoms similar to ADHD. This is just another reason to reduce your screen time and, more importantly, that of your children.

> **Self-Care:** Taking care of one's body involves self-care activities promoting relaxation and stress management. This includes taking regular breaks, indulging in healthy hobbies, spending time outdoors, and prioritizing activities that bring you joy and fulfillment.

APPLY

At this point, you may feel like you've been reliving a ninth-grade health class. It is hard to commit to learning about the essentials of physical health when there are so many quick and easy health "fixes" available around each corner. Well, guess what? They don't work. We must teach our children to apply the necessities of physical intelligence early on so it becomes habitual rather than an add-on to their busy lives.

This section tests a person's skill at applying what they have learned about physical development. Getting healthy is a long process. Remembering the details and understanding the impacts of health are the easy parts. Application is where the rubber meets the road.

In the quest for a healthy life, a critical triad of habits—exercise, nutrition, and sleep—stands as the cornerstone of well-being (see Figure 5.3). The three elements come only with effort and require commitment. Often intertwined, they are essential pillars upon which a robust and vibrant life is built. Let's delve into the significance of actively participating in exercise, eating right, and ensuring sufficient sleep and explore how they synergistically contribute to overall health and vitality.

Figure 5.3. Triad of Health

Exercise: Energize Your Body and Mind

Exercise is not merely a means to sculpt a body and look good at the beach; it is vital to maintaining optimal physical health. The benefits of regular physical activity extend far beyond the confines of the gym or the track.

The hard part is maintaining motivation in the long term. If you have never heard of Dr. Ogie Shaw, look him up on YouTube. He gives fantastic TEDx talks. Besides being hilarious, he is honest and provides some of the best advice I have listened to regarding lifelong exercise. After offering some sobering statistics on childhood obesity, Dr. Shaw speaks to why we are so unlikely to exercise. The most common excuses, he says, are:

1. "I don't have time."
2. "I'm too lazy to do it even when I have the time." That one gets a good laugh.

So, how do we stay motivated? Well, many programs tell you how much fun exercise is, but truthfully, exercise done correctly isn't always fun. "Intensity, duration, and frequency are critical to your success," says Dr. Shaw.[5] So here is some truthful and realistic advice.

1. To avoid falling back into poor exercise habits, it's essential to establish a routine for five consecutive years. That requires a significant commitment! Remember when you were young and ran around just for the joy of it? Imagine being able to maintain that feeling throughout your entire life. We need to help our children make that same connection.
2. Work out most days in some form or fashion. Many recommendations suggest three days a week, but since motivation is the issue, three days allows you too much opportunity to put it off. A person will likely say, "I'll work out tomorrow," but tomorrow never comes. Consistency is the key.
3. According to Dr. Shaw, if you work out first thing in the morning, the likelihood of remaining consistent improves by 300 percent.[6] Work out at a time when you have more control over your schedule. For children, that is typically after school, so maybe plan some run time before homework begins.
4. Limit workouts to twenty minutes or fewer to reduce injury risk and increase the likelihood of repetition.
5. Work against resistance. Have children use their own body weight so they don't injure themselves with excessive weights and actions. Have them try to tire themselves as quickly as possible.

There are no quick fixes to achieving physical greatness. I suggest you have your child try their best every day. Small victories add up.

Nutrition: Fuel Your Body, Nourish Your Soul

The adage "you are what you eat" holds true when considering the importance of nutrition in maintaining overall health. Our food fuels our bodies. It provides the essential nutrients for growth, repair, and function.

By prioritizing nutrient-dense foods and adopting healthy eating habits, a person can nourish their body and mind, promoting a state of vigor and resilience from within.

Dr. Shaw has a great deal to say on this topic as well.

1. Never diet! (great news for a change)—"Eat for nutrition, never for weight loss, and never give up foods you aren't willing to give up forever."[7]
2. Stay hydrated—it keeps a person full and is great for your body. Have your child carry a water container at school.
3. Make your child eat breakfast.
4. Include protein in most meals.

Sleep: Recharge and Renew

Prioritizing sufficient sleep is not a luxury. It's a necessity for optimal health and performance. Creating a conducive sleep environment, practicing relaxation techniques, and establishing a consistent sleep schedule contribute to better sleep hygiene and overall well-being.

There are a variety of sleep aids on the market, but my two favorites are light and music, especially for children. I recommend a bedroom light projector (I have one that produces something akin to the aurora borealis) and the use of classical music or ambient sounds of rain, running water, wind, fire, etc. When a person adds these sleep aids to their routine and, importantly, puts their phone away, they enable their mind to relax. With practice, one's mind, now tranquil, will be able to process any issues they are facing while they sleep.

In the intricate tapestry of human health, the threads of exercise, nutrition, and sleep are tightly woven, each contributing its unique hue to the vibrant mosaic of well-being. By actively participating in training, eating right, and ensuring sufficient sleep, one can cultivate a foundation of health that empowers a person to thrive.

ANALYZE

Once you have applied what you have learned about physical development, you can step back and examine the concepts in more detail, reflecting on how they work in practice. By analyzing these elements at the level of their constituent parts, you can grasp the degree of their impact and see how they interrelate. Let's analyze what happens to a body when a person works out, eats right, and gets the necessary sleep. You might be surprised how the body, much like the brain, adapts to those actions.

Exercise

Regular physical exercise triggers a cascade of physiological changes within the body, leading to visible and internal transformations.

- Increased blood flow to muscles and tissues occurs, causing them to receive more oxygen and nutrients, improving repair. Over time, muscle fibers undergo hypertrophy, resulting in increased muscle mass and tone. It is important for children to understand why muscle development is important.

- Concurrently, bone density improves.
- Regular workouts also stimulate the release of endorphins, the neurotransmitters responsible for feelings of euphoria and pain reduction, and contribute to improved mood and mental well-being. Children don't always understand the relationship between exercise and mental health. So, remind them.
- Cardiovascular function improves as the heart becomes more efficient at pumping blood. The result is a lower resting heart rate and improved endurance.
- Exercise promotes better sleep patterns, an enhanced metabolism, and a more efficient immune system. All this culminates in a healthier, more vibrant physique and increased overall vitality.

Have you ever been talking with your child after a long stint of television bingeing, internet surfing, or gaming? They tend to be irritable, socially disconnected, intellectually sluggish, and sometimes ethically compromised. This is exactly what happens when they are sedentary for too long. As my parents would say, "Go outside and play."

Nutrition
Nutrition has similar positive impacts to working out. The food children eat directly affects the health of their bodies. A balanced diet fuels the body with nutrients essential to optimal functioning and macronutrients—carbohydrates, proteins, and fats—essential to cellular repair and energy production.

- Carbohydrates are broken down into glucose, providing immediate energy.
- Proteins aid muscle repair and growth.
- Fats, when consumed in moderation, support hormone production and assist in absorbing fat-soluble vitamins.
- Micronutrients, such as vitamins and minerals, are crucial in various physiological processes. For instance, vitamin C supports immune function, vitamin D aids in calcium absorption for bone health, and iron is essential for oxygen transport in the blood.

As you can see, everything we eat has a specific purpose. I urge you to be intentional about what you feed your child. Think consciously about what and how they consume food. Many of us, like myself, consume without thinking about what we eat. We don't pay attention to our choices or portion size.

I don't know about you, but I fall into the "eat in front of the TV" trap. My passion for sports is legendary: Cleveland Browns, Guardians, Cavaliers, and Ohio State Buckeyes. While I'm watching my teams, I have a tendency to munch distractedly and fail to adhere to reasonable portions. If this resonates with you, it's essential to be careful and take steps to teach your child to eat mindfully.

As a starting point, I challenge you to give your child a smaller portion of food to start. If they need more, they can have it. However, adding more to their plate requires them to do so consciously. It forces their brain to ask the question, "Do I need more?" It interrupts the process of mindless eating. Once you've mastered this first technique, try the following steps:

- Consider *what* you are about to serve. If healthy and adequately portioned, serve freely.
- If you serve something less healthy, take less to start, and then, before refilling their dish, ask yourself whether they actually need more.
- If they are given a significant portion, such as at a restaurant, try not to allow them to eat it mindlessly (without listening to their body's hunger cues). Have them pay attention so they know when they are full. This also helps slow them down, which gives their body a chance to feel satiated.
- If they are a Browns fan, seek help immediately. I don't have a cure for this.

Sleep

Sleep profoundly influences cognitive function, memory formation, and overall mental clarity. Proper sleep is also associated with improved mood, as it enables the brain to process emotions effectively and reduces the likelihood of depression and anxiety. Clearly, sleep not only supports the health of the body but also rewires the brain for optimal functioning.

Here is an example of rewiring. When I was younger, I loved the game Tetris.[8] I would play for hours on end. I remember dreaming about the falling colorful blocks and stacking them properly. My brain recognized that the game was part of my life and worked to enhance my skills while I slept.

However, this skill development bled into my everyday life too. My mom asked me to go to the store with her one day. She found me pulling every cereal box forward so each row was flush. She asked me what I was doing, to which I replied, "I don't know; I just like them this way." My subconscious mind was at work, trying a new skill I had learned. To this day, I still compulsively organize things on my desk in straight lines. Thank you, Tetris!

EVALUATE

Evaluating progress is a central part of physical development. It does not need to be overly complicated, but you should record a child's growth to validate their progress or find and assess patterns so as to refine a strategy. I have a reMarkable 2, the Digital Paper Tablet, to organize everything in my life. I keep track of my tasks related to school, my chapters for this book, and my health records, including my eating habits, workout routine, and sleep records.

Be sure to consider your child's habits of nutrition, sleep, and exercise. If your child is showing a deficiency, please address it immediately.

CREATE

All I ask is that you do your best, and forget the rest.
—Tony Horton[9]

The highest level of learning, creation, is reserved for those who reach rarified air. They have mastered the information required to understand the development of physical health and have achieved a level of physical intelligence. They have applied concepts of exercise, nutrition, and sleep to their everyday life. They regularly analyze their program, including its impacts, and evaluate their progress. Not only that, but they have taken a leap beyond these first five levels to create a new and unique program to enhance health for themselves, and possibly others.

I can't tell you how to invent a new program. Otherwise, I would have made a lot of money doing it myself. Instead, I will highlight a special individual who has accomplished the task, inspiring my friend Tommy along the way.

Tony Horton is a renowned fitness trainer, author, and the creator of the popular P90X workout program. Born on July 2, 1967, in Rhode Island, he developed a passion for fitness at a young age, which blossomed into a lifelong career. He first gained recognition in the 1990s as a personal trainer, helping a variety of clients achieve their fitness goals.

In 2003, Horton launched P90X, a revolutionary ninety-day home fitness program based on the pioneering concept of "muscle confusion." The workout series combines strength training, cardio, yoga, and plyometrics into a challenging regime designed to maximize results in a short period. Combining a variety of different exercises keeps the body guessing, prevents fitness plateaus, and promotes continuous improvement.

Horton is known for his high-energy approach and motivational style that make workouts both enjoyable and effective. His programs, subsequent series, live events, and social media have garnered millions of fans worldwide and transformed countless lives. In addition to P90X, Horton has authored several books focused on fitness, nutrition, and wellness, including *Bring It!* and *The Big Picture: 11 Laws That Will Change Your Life*.[10]

Have you created a workout routine, nutrition program, and sleep schedule that are unique to your child's needs and goals?

I can't provide the perfect plan for your child, but I hope you commit to enhancing their physical well-being to the fullest.

SUMMARY

- Modern Western society is in the midst of a health crisis, and it is incumbent upon those who understand this to push back on the causes of this decline, including misguided educational trends, media, and social media.
- Our physical health has a direct impact on our brain health, which affects our cognitive function and well-being.
- We are offered a lot of quick fixes using simple methods, but these don't provide long-lasting and sustainable change. As always, complex problems require complex solutions. Improving our physical health requires small, incremental steps toward a goal until one reaches a tipping point.
- The critical elements to focus on in a plan are adequate sleep, good nutrition, and plenty of exercise.
- Use Bloom's Taxonomy to memorize, understand, apply, analyze, evaluate, and create so you can master your physical health, turning it into physical intelligence.

CHAPTER SIX

INTELLECTUAL DEVELOPMENT

*Education is not the learning of the facts,
but the training of the mind to think.*
—Albert Einstein[1]

IT'S NEVER TOO LATE TO CHANGE OUR PATH

In a typical 1970s second-grade classroom, a small boy, no more than seven, sat nervously at an old wooden desk. The late-spring sun filtered through the windows, reminding the students that summer was almost upon them. Most students looked forward to the upcoming summer swims, playground visits, and family vacations; however, the young boy had yet to let his mind wander to the festive days ahead because one more academic hurdle remained. A final reading test.

He prayed for a miracle, his fingers gripping one another and dripping with sweat. He was dreading the impossible task ahead. He watched helplessly as students were asked to read for the teacher at the front of the room. The boy silently hoped the teacher would skip over him, yet the relentless call of names continued. It was the end of the second-grade year and time for another reading evaluation. The boy knew it was his last chance to move to third grade with his friends.

One by one, students shuffled to the front and read one of the standard passages, then skipped back to their seats with a smile. Most of the students had performed well throughout the year. For them, the exercise was a mere formality. When the young boy looked up, his kind and supportive teacher was sitting at her desk, smiling. She was proud of herself and the students who had proven their worth, and she looked at them like Saint Peter at the Pearly Gates upon the admission of another venerated soul.

He heard his name like a roll of distant thunder. The teacher's smile, while welcoming, looked artificial—almost sad. He stood, his heart racing, and looked at his friend in the adjacent seat, but he was too nervous to return his gaze. Desperately wanting to escape, the young boy momentarily thought about dashing out the door and fleeing. Instead, he marched forward and prepared to confront the evaluation of his intellect, whether it was success or failure.

The teacher handed him the passage to read. He struggled excruciatingly through every syllable and sentence in his ineptitude but kept going. When he looked up, he noticed his friend leaning forward, almost imploring the words to come, but he continued to stumble and mispronounce. Finally, he finished. He looked at the teacher with tears in his eyes. The teacher looked solemnly at him, lowered her head, and guided him back to his seat. The boy knew his buddy, Bob, would be moving on to third grade—and he knew he would be saying goodbye.

The years dragged along. Lacking confidence and intellect, and without any particular physical gifts, the boy was terrified to stand out. He measured every year not by his accomplishments but by his failures—one after another. But he kept grinding. Teacher after teacher asked him to memorize this or that, yet each time, much like those words in second grade, his brain would not retain or recall the information. Each time a teacher called on him, anxiety pounded him, and he stumbled with every answer.

Once he became a young man, he still hid in the back of classrooms, stayed quiet, and hoped to get by without repeating another year of school. If someone had asked him why he continued, he might have answered, "What else should I have done?" As most of us do, he followed the prescribed educational path from early childhood to young adulthood, without asking questions or understanding why he attended.

High school graduation approached. With a 2.2 grade point average, a disappointing athletic career, and the prospect of an upcoming job in a factory shipping department, he resigned himself to mediocrity. Despite this, he kept asking, "What is the purpose of all of this?"

A year and a half after high school, while working in an industrial park, the young man looked around one fateful day. Five other workers piled boxes atop one another. Everyone did their duties, but each man's face bore a look of discontentment and sadness. The young man's mind overflowed with a pervasive sense of loss. He went home, sat on the edge of his bed, and wept softly as he mourned what felt like the death of hope. The following day, however, he awoke with renewed determination—he would find a way to return to school and try to change his fate.

I am sure you have figured out by now that the boy was me. That night of great sadness and desperation was my call to adventure. Up to that point, I had found a lot of reasons not to try and change direction, but I had never abandoned my faint vision of a different and better path. I could not predict the future, but I knew I did not want my ordinary life.

My early experiences reflect the journey of many children today. They attend school day after day, often without grasping its significance or purpose. This lack of understanding can lead some children to resent both their schools and teachers, fostering a combative environment. Consequently, teachers may become worn down, and the stresses affecting the children can be passed on to them, creating a negative culture devoid of purpose.

Children must understand from an early age that intellectual development represents the path to true wisdom. Once mastered, it allows you to become the advice giver, opinion maker, and mentor. Just as the peak of physical fitness allows one to master the longevity of life, the power of intellect enables one to fully understand one's existence. Once understood, a child can begin unlocking the mysteries of the universe and the infinite knowledge it offers.

A HISTORY OF OUR INTELLECT: RISE AND FALL

Since the mid-1800s, education has encouraged people to achieve the American Dream. Schools have long been equipped to teach verbal, numerical, and general knowledge. Sadly, not everyone was included at this time due to our original sin of slavery and lack of female rights. While I will not go into detail here, these facts should be recognized as an initial condition of our history. Remember what we discussed in Chapter 4—initial conditions can cause significant differences in outcomes.

Education became compulsory in 1918 based on the need for an educated public to serve as industry laborers. While schooling in the early twentieth century promoted remembering basic facts and understanding concepts, the higher levels of thinking were modestly promoted and mostly reserved for the elite. In essence, they wanted people smart enough to run the machines but not so bright as to bring about change. In many ways, the workers were seen as tools of industry, not as people.

The old philosophy boiled down to "I pay you to work, not think."

Then along came John Dewey in the late nineteenth century, who was ahead of his time in educational theory. Dewey promoted the ideal of nurturing critical thought through learning, focusing on the fundamentals of the core four subjects, but he also encouraged advancements in social, emotional, ethical, and physical intelligence along with the required intellectual skills. His message did not gain immediate traction, and I am afraid we are still catching up to his genius. However, his philosophy still guides both public and private schools today.

Although I am in the private education sector, my public school colleagues entered the educational profession for the same altruistic reasons: to help young people achieve their holistic capacity. It is one of the most noble professions one can join. I greatly admire everyone who has authentically worked with children, especially in today's tumultuous environment.

It must be said that the educational system must have been doing something right over this period. In the last century, IQ scores have gone up about two to three points per decade, climbing a total of thirty points. To move an entire nation up thirty points in over a century is equivalent to shifting the whole population two standard deviations upward, or in straightforward terms, moving them on average from borderline impaired, one stage above disability, to average intelligence. That is a remarkable achievement and one for which a nation of teachers should be proud. Below, you can see the IQ scale, which explains how IQ scores relate to mental aptitude.

- 1 to 24: Profound mental disability
- 25 to 39: Severe mental disability
- 40 to 54: Moderate mental disability
- **55 to 79: Borderline impaired**
- 80 to 89: Low average
- **85 to 114: Average intelligence**
- 115 to 129: Above average or bright
- 130 to 144: Moderately gifted
- 145 to 159: Highly gifted

However, for the first time since we have tracked intelligence, our ability as a nation may be in decline. In the last decade, IQ has dipped two points. Given our progress in the last century, this is particularly alarming and poignant. I believe this is due to the chaotic interrupters, which I highlighted early on in the book and which will continue to be relevant in later chapters.

Much like our understanding of the country's recent decay in relation to physical development, we must take proactive measures to address the alarming trends in intellectual loss. We should urgently define what is contributing to our decline and discover how to change these patterns. I can promise you that it is not a teaching problem.

THE DAMAGE DONE BY MODERN TECHNOLOGY

At my current school, we are in a unique situation. We do not have direct cell service but maintain a robust internal communication system for safety and security. All technology is filtered and monitored through our highly secure network. This ensures that our technology use is highly restricted—tech is used only as a practical tool, as intended. As such, the students cannot use their phones, and all their technology use is controlled because they have school-issued iPads. It's akin to an (unintended) educational experiment.

As a result, our students cannot use social media within our walls, and they, therefore, experience no negative impacts from it while at school. I am not suggesting that they do not use it outside of school, but for this reason, we have begun to work with families, asking parents to hold off getting their children smart technology until after eighth grade.

I recently hosted a family coffee at my school to talk about technology and how it interrupts children's development. As part of the conversation, one astute parent mentioned the following about technology as a tool:

> We have always been told that technology is just a tool that can be used for good or for ill. There is a level of truth to this: when I give my children a plastic hammer, they pick up the tool and use it to knock the blocks through a wooden table (as intended) or bonk their sister on the head (unintended). They can build, or they can break. But unlike the phone, the hammer is not addictive. It does not call them to use it over and over. Eventually, they get bored of the toy hammer and put it down. They don't do that with their phones.
>
> —Dan Saxton

This was a paradigm-shifting insight. While technology is often recognized as just a tool, its highly addictive and adaptive properties mean it goes far beyond this definition. And social media is a particularly nefarious example. Not even gaming, which can be highly addictive, carries the same impact. Social media mixes a combination of false physical attributes (filters), faceless social connections, the fostering of emotional fragility, ethical deception, and intellectual falsities. And all of this is intentionally embedded in the technology to keep children clicking and scrolling. It is hard enough for adults to combat its lure; imagine the appeal to an impressionable adolescent with a developing mind. It has fostered an entire "click-bait" society.

This type of technology also creates echo chambers. As you have probably recognized, social media uses algorithms to calculate what a person looks at and for how long. If a child pauses momentarily while scrolling, the algorithm recognizes their interest and provides like-minded content. Have you ever noticed that when you look up a political story or request information on it from your digital assistant, that same perspective begins to appear across all of your digital platforms?

This encourages us to believe in only one viewpoint, and we wonder why we are radicalized to unhealthy levels. It is an example of a convenience of the mind. True intellect encourages us to listen to both sides of a debate and then, when fully understood, make an informed decision. Social media is working directly against this age-old proven method.

And it's only getting worse. Businesses have seen the power of this type of manipulative behavior and have been swayed to utilize it to their advantage. News outlets used to be the checks and balances of society. Now, the news outlets seem to have chosen their political and cultural sides and are part of the problem—promoting echo chambers. I am sorry to say that economic survival has influenced our broadcasters. Instead of reporting unbiased and informational news, they seek to attract a population of loyal watchers by peddling what they want to hear, all to sell advertising. It is a disturbing trend.

I don't want to rant but rather recognize that this behavior works against teaching intellect as an attribute. Be cautious when choosing a side without thoroughly researching the situation and the reason for each side's discontent. Try to be led by facts and the desire for objectivity rather than your emotions. Avoid these pitfalls within yourself and your children when trying to achieve a vision. Here are a few more elements to consider when looking at how modern technology is interrupting our intellectual development.

Our modern world has evolved around the concept of convenience, leveraging intelligent technologies to automate various tasks. So far, these technologies have primarily addressed mundane chores, such as robotic vacuum cleaners like Roomba, virtual assistants like Alexa and Google Assistant for playing music or providing basic information, and GPS systems that have replaced traditional maps. While these advancements have made some daily activities easier, their overall impact has been limited. However, we must acknowledge a key reality: Anything that can be automated will eventually be automated. The pressing question now is: To what extent will this automation occur?

Let's take one of the newer technologies—AI language and art models. Given I am using Grammarly, I believe there is an appropriate time and place to use it; however, I worry young people will utilize programs to the detriment of their own creativity and intellectual growth, potentially stifling brain development. The AI creation of documents (ChatGPT), Art (OpenAI—Dall-E 2), and Film (OpenAI—Sora), for example, may lead us to withdraw from creating within these disciplines altogether, losing our skills and ability to produce anything new or unique. Ultimately, this could stifle our evolution as a species. Allow me an example.

When a young person learns to drive a car, they must become proficient before earning a license. Let's imagine a student getting into a new vehicle. The instructor tells the student to drive back and forth to the local Walmart. Do you think it would be justified for the student to hit a few buttons and allow the car to steer on autopilot? Did the young person learn how to drive? Indeed, does a young person really learn to write, calculate, and draw if they used these adaptive technologies during their formative years? You might say that the end result is the same, so it doesn't matter. This is true enough, but their brains weren't being challenged and developed during these processes, so it still has a tangible impact with worrying results.

Do you see an impact of automated technology within yourself, your family, or schools?

How is it good?

How is it bad?

I don't feel families and schools give the impact of these technologies sufficient consideration. In an online seminar recently, an expert proclaimed that AI is no different from calculators. I found the statement overly simplistic. The calculator only allows a person to move through the first three levels of Bloom's taxonomy—Remember, Understand, and Apply a problem—and only with direct input from the user. However, ChatGPT not only remembers, understands, and solves an issue; it can then quickly analyze, evaluate, and create something novel.

I am not suggesting a ban on AI intelligence, but we must be careful with the level and timing of implementation. Young students should not use these tools before they learn the basic skills that will nurture their young brains. Indeed, as you better yourself, you should not rely on this technology until you have become proficient in a skill yourself.

If you have not had a chance to see the movie *WALL-E*, a provocative and potentially prophetic film, I highly suggest it.[2] In *WALL-E*, the human experience is portrayed as disconnected and unsustainable. Humans live in a spaceship where every need is met by machines, leading to intellectual, social, emotional, ethical, and physical deterioration. Ultimately, the people rediscover their humanity through interactions with WALL-E, a loving little robot. The film emphasizes the need for genuine human connection, development, and the rejection of convenience. This might be a window into the impact of these trends on intellectual loss and where we could end up if we don't make changes.

As we've seen, as convenience increases, we decline intellectually and succumb to manipulation; we lose a little more of our humanity daily. I encourage people to embrace their learning to combat this. It represents a skill of immense value. We have already seen the impact of convenience on physical health (rampant obesity) and are now beginning to see it in intellect (a drop in overall intelligence). In future chapters, we will see how it's degrading our social skills, emotional health, and ethical standards, as well.

Now, let's dig into the basics of intellectual development.

APPLYING BLOOM'S TAXONOMY TO INTELLECTUAL DEVELOPMENT

REMEMBER

Below are the essential elements of intellectual understanding for which we can test. I will do my best to keep this information as concise as possible. I suggest you read through the list and consider which strengths and challenges you have.

- **Verbal Comprehension:** verbal reasoning, vocabulary, comprehension, and fluency.
- **Visual-Spatial Abilities:** understanding and interpreting visual information, mental rotation, spatial reasoning, and visual memory.
- **Working Memory:** your ability to hold and temporarily manipulate information in the mind.
- **Processing Speed:** how quickly you can process and respond to information.
- **Executive Functioning:** higher-order cognitive processes such as planning, problem-solving, inhibition, mental flexibility, and decision-making.
- **Attention:** your ability to focus, sustain attention, divide attention, and selectively attend to relevant information while ignoring distractions.
- **Logical and Abstract Reasoning:** your ability to think logically, make inferences, identify patterns, and solve abstract problems.
- **Numerical Abilities:** skills related to numerical reasoning, mathematical problem-solving, arithmetic operations, and quantitative reasoning.
- **Memory Functioning:** your abilities in relation to short-term, long-term, episodic, semantic, and working memory.
- **General Knowledge:** your knowledge across various domains, including history, science, literature, geography, and current events.

Wow, our brains do a lot more than we think, don't they? Or as my concept editor, Art Fogartie, points out, "More than for wearing a hat."

Educators understand that starting knowledge development in the earliest grade levels is essential. Children who aspire to read, write, and think mathematically need to grasp the foundational elements of these subjects in order to later achieve a deeper understanding of language and mathematics.

In essence, *what* we learn pales in comparison to *why* we learn.

For instance, let's consider mathematics.

When I was teaching middle school Algebra I and II, students frequently posed the age-old question, "Dr. Strecker, when will we ever use this stuff?" In my early years, I typically referred to careers in mathematics like science, engineering, and technology. Then, to appease the non-STEM students, I would usually rely on restaurant tips or estimating a car loan. Still, all of those answers were insufficient. After honestly thinking about the greater purpose of learning, I feel I have developed sufficient answers for the students.

Let's consider the purpose of our math and ELA subject areas and how each refines the brain's processing acumen:

Math is the language of logic and rationality. When we process math problems, our brain rewires to think more logically, creating a biological framework of systems and process thinking. Countless professions use this approach. When doctors decipher the root cause of symptoms, they eliminate possible origins to reach a diagnosis. Judges must listen to case facts to determine a final verdict. Mathematical thinking—even outside of mathematical disciplines—is the process by which we arrive—via predictable, logic-based pathways, at precise and certain conclusions. It engages complex variables to lead us sensibly to reliable and reasonable closure. Math isn't just about math, but rather a way to structure our brains.

Language Arts: Human beings have evolved to become the dominant species on the planet. This is certainly due to something other than our size and strength, as we know there are bigger and stronger animals that live among us. Communication has played a significant role in advancing our species. The ability to communicate and form successful social groups has elevated our species above all others. Whatever the genre—poetry, oral storytelling, written scientific documentation, song, or prayer, all forms of communication convey information to others. One's ability to communicate effectively has a direct correlation to future success.

And this is just two of countless areas of study.

Now, look back over the functions of the brain above. Immediately, you will begin to connect how the core subjects we teach nurture complex brain functions in children.

UNDERSTAND

I know that I am intelligent because I know that I know nothing.
—SOCRATES[3]

Intellectual development encompasses a vast array of concepts and ideas, making it impossible to remember and fully understand everything. Each aspect of brain function mentioned can serve as a distinct area of study within psychology or education.

Let's explore these topics in greater detail:

Verbal Comprehension is essential for understanding and expressing ideas effectively. It supports communication and learning in academic and real-world contexts, leading to more transparent interactions and deeper connections.

It is only possible to lead in life if you have the ability to communicate your message clearly. The more words you know, the more precise you can be with your language. Have you ever listened to a gifted presenter? You hang on their words as they weave their story like a beautiful tapestry. Mastering the ability to use meaningful language is fundamental to bringing an idea to fruition. I suggest you encourage your children to vary and expand their vocabulary.

Visual-Spatial Abilities are vital for understanding and navigating the world around you. By improving spatial awareness and problem-solving abilities, they support tasks like map reading, spatial reasoning, and creative endeavors. These skills are crucial in architecture, engineering, and art.

To appreciate life to the fullest, you use a combination of what you see and what you can imagine. Look at something sitting in front of you right now. Imagine picking up the object and rotating it 360 degrees. Now visualize it twice its size, a different color, etc. That mental ability is essential to develop. Whether it be making art, redecorating your home, or imagining a world beyond this one, the ability to create is imperative.

Working Memory speaks to the brain's ability to hold on to and manipulate information needed for problem-solving and decision-making. It approximates a mental workspace where we process and use information in real time, which leads to better learning and cognitive performance.

If you are older, do you recall your home phone number from childhood? I'm guessing, with little effort, you are likely to remember yours and possibly those of your friends or family members. In today's age, when exchanging numbers, we don't even attempt to remember a ten-number sequence. It immediately goes into our phones as a new contact. This skill, due to convenience technology, has declined. However, those who can readily remember and recall information on the spot are demonstrating this important component of intelligence. This is still a valuable skill we need to promote in children.

Processing Speed refers to how quickly someone can take in and respond to information. It's essential for tasks like problem-solving and learning. Fast processing speed leads to efficient cognitive function and better performance in various areas of life.

You probably didn't realize your brain has a speed limit. We see this in young children all the time. It might manifest as a delay in learning or the ability to respond promptly. The good news is that, like many cognitive abilities, practice can improve it. You can experience this in a variety of different ways.

My wife and I flew down to Orlando to pick up our son and help move him home. Before we returned, we decided to attend a Warrant concert. (Yes, I graduated from high school in 1989, so I like hair bands.) Whenever a song began, my son turned to me. He expected me to come up with the song's title. Surprisingly, the tune's names popped into my head before anyone started singing the lyrics. That ability is processing speed. Each song reminded me of a memory from earlier in my life. "Uncle Tom's Cabin" reminded me of fishing with Sean and Bob on the Olentangy River in Columbus, Ohio.[4] I am not sure remembering Warrant songs will be overly valuable, but the ability to recall information quickly is vital in leadership— so let's call it good practice.

Executive Functioning is a mental skill that helps you plan and manage tasks efficiently. It encompasses cognitive flexibility, working memory, impulse control, and task initiation. It plays a crucial role in your daily life, including in decision-making and self-regulation. If you have well-developed executive function skills, you are better equipped to succeed intellectually, emotionally, and socially.

The Stanford Marshmallow Test is a psychological experiment conducted by psychologist Walter Mischel in the late 1960s and early 1970s. It is a favorite of mine on YouTube (look it up).[5] You will laugh, I promise. The study assessed children's ability to delay gratification and serves as a predictor of their future success. In the test, a child was offered a choice between eating one marshmallow immediately or waiting for a short period (typically fifteen minutes) to receive two marshmallows. However, the first marshmallow was put on a plate in front of them, and they had to resist eating it.

The test revealed that children who could delay gratification and wait for the larger reward had better outcomes later in life, such as higher SAT scores, educational attainment, and social competence. The Marshmallow Test has since become famous for its insights into self-control and the importance of delayed gratification in achieving long-term goals. It reflects high executive functioning because it relates to the ability to plan ahead to improve your results and ignore your primal impulses.

My favorite part of the video involves watching the children's faces while they manage this internal struggle. They sniff, lick, and play with the marshmallows. Many try various strategies to control their desire to eat the sweets. Of course, a few immediately stuff the marshmallow into their mouth and enjoy the sugar rush with no regret. You've got to love children.

Attention is a fundamental cognitive process crucial in nearly every aspect of human life. It allows us to focus on relevant information while filtering out distractions and enabling effective learning. Attention is essential for maintaining concentration during tasks, whether studying or engaging in conversations.

I have always enjoyed working individually with students as a school administrator. As you know, I struggled with academic work when I was younger, so it's particularly satisfying to help them reach their potential. Occasionally, I encounter a student who learns better when working one-on-one. It often has nothing to do with the teacher or class. Instead, the student reacts better in a situation that requires their undivided attention. The students I have worked with often claim they are mentally exhausted at the end of the session as they are not used to such intense concentration. But just like a runner must exercise to increase stamina, the mind must focus for extended periods to increase its attention. Without stamina, the student is often unfairly labeled lazy or lacking in intelligence.

Logical and Abstract Reasoning are essential cognitive skills that enable you to analyze complex problems, make informed decisions, and navigate the world with clarity and precision. Thank you, math!

Logical thinking involves identifying patterns, deducing relationships, and drawing valid conclusions based on evidence and reasoning.

Abstract thinking, on the other hand, allows you to conceptualize ideas, think creatively, and envision possibilities beyond our concrete reality. These skills facilitate critical thinking and innovation in various domains, including science, mathematics, engineering, and philosophy.

Logical and abstract reasoning relates to the higher-level attributes of Bloom's Taxonomy—analysis, evaluation, and creation. Leaders and visionaries are able to apply rational thought processes in emotionally charged moments. Given individuals in our culture sometimes use emotions in nefarious ways, many times to manipulate you, it is essential to focus on logic in these moments.

Numerical Abilities are crucial for interpreting data and making decisions. They enhance logical reasoning and allow you to navigate quantitative information effectively, from budgeting to scientific analysis, which leads to better problem-solving abilities.

Being a math teacher, I love data and statistics. Annually, I cross-reference each student's ability level (OLSAT) and compare it to their math and English (ERB) performance scores. The differential provides the school with the necessary metrics to ensure each child achieves at their capacity and, in many cases, beyond it. This is part of the evaluative process in Bloom's Taxonomy. Anyone can say they have a great school or family, but the claim becomes more substantial when you can verify the proclamation with objective evidence. It is not always possible to evaluate each element of success numerically, but I encourage you to find ways when possible.

At Valley School, we evaluate not only intellectual achievement (ability compared to performance) but also social and emotional wellness, ethical behavior, and physical fitness. All five intelligences are included in our evaluative matrix.

Memory Function is crucial for everyday tasks, from recalling important information to learning new skills. It enables you to store, retain, and retrieve information, drawing on past experiences and knowledge, supporting learning, and contributing to overall cognitive functioning. It also plays a significant role in maintaining relationships and navigating daily routines.

This goes back to my earlier suggestion on memory development. Have you ever been at a gathering when someone you may have only met once comes up and welcomes you by name? That is the power of memory. You are immediately impressed by someone who can remember details about you and your life, and this can strengthen your bond. It takes practice to force your brain to consciously remember facts in conversation rather than merely responding.

I once used the following strategy at an event. I walked in deciding that I was only there to ask questions and get to know everyone as best I could. I did not respond with my own thoughts the whole evening. Questions only! Funnily enough, when I walked out, my wife said someone had told her I was the best conversationalist he had ever met. Try this approach one evening. You will like the results.

General Knowledge represents the cornerstone of our understanding of the world. It facilitates social interactions and promotes personal growth. Continuously expanding our general knowledge empowers us to engage meaningfully with the world around us and make informed contributions to society.

Given the infinite topics in our world, with even more to come, I can only offer two recommendations:

1. Commit to being a lifelong learner.
2. Transition away from mindless entertainment, such as bingeing TV programs, scrolling through social media, and video gaming. Instead, use the time to activate your mind through conscious learning via books, documentaries, and YouTube videos (technology isn't all bad). The more knowledge you consume, the more helpful you can be to yourself—and your children.

APPLY

At the beginning of the chapter, I shared my story of intellectual struggle as a child. Once I made the decision to go back to college, the next tipping point was a psychology class that opened my eyes to my true potential. You see, that was the moment I realized that my brain could begin to reshape itself to my will. The advice I am about to share with you is the next step.

Imagine you just bought a brand-new car. Personally, I would love one of those beautiful Italian sports cars; unfortunately, I don't fit in them. No matter what kind of car you choose, you set out to learn the names of its parts—tires, doors, radiators, gas tanks—once memorized, you can identify each part, attaching the memory to a purpose (and now you've mastered the first level of Bloom's Taxonomy).

Next, you attach understanding to each car part. Tires are used to rotate to allow the car to move. Doors open and close to let you get in and out. Before you know it, you know what each part does and why. This is the second level of Bloom's Taxonomy.

However, now you need to apply this knowledge and understanding. To do this, you need to take action.

In the example of the car, you get in, put on your seat belt, start it up, put the car in drive, and press gently on the accelerator, starting to move down the road. I hope you are beginning to understand the intellectual leap required. The process may feel a bit awkward as you navigate the application process for the first time. Day after day, you practice getting better at controlling the vehicle. Before you know it, you are driving without thinking about it at all.

What you may have realized is that you really didn't need to know the parts and understand what the parts do to successfully drive the car. However, that foundation of knowledge gives you a deeper understanding and skill level when it comes to interacting with the car and overcoming problems.

Imagine you're driving along one day, and you hear a soft bang. You pull over and shut off the car to listen more intently. You hear nothing new. You try to restart it, but nothing happens. Not even a click. For those with no knowledge or understanding of their car, they are stranded and reliant on someone else's help. However, given you know the parts and their functions and given nothing is happening, you deduce it might be electrical. You pop the hood and look at the battery. Sure enough, one of the connectors has detached. A quick fix, and you are back on the road.

Similarly, if you know the various components of intelligence and what they are used for, you appreciate their importance, especially when used at advanced levels. Everyone has a brain, and we all learn to apply it. If you use it to scroll the low-level content on Facebook, your brain will oblige and become better at it (and worse at processing high-level content). Conversely, if you spend time reading advanced material in challenging books, your brain will adapt accordingly and you will keep developing.

Let's return to the car example. If you only spend time driving in a parking lot (low-level, easy driving), you will limit your ability to drive effectively on the interstate. If you practice in varied environments, however, you will reach the pinnacle of your driving prowess. I suppose an extreme example of an expert driver might be a Formula I racer—*I knew there was a reason I loved those Italian sports cars.*

So far, you have learned the components of intelligence and you understand why each component is important. You should now begin to apply this knowledge accordingly to yourself and your children. Where one goes next will begin to refine one's overall wisdom.

Intelligence is even more malleable than your physique. One's brain is not just primed for learning, it craves it. All one needs to do is feed it. Use what I have mentioned in the remembering and understanding sections of intellect to improve memory, processing speed, attention, logic, etc. Consider what one must *apply* to increase one's intellect and achieve one's vision. Once you understand these levels, you will become highly skilled at analyzing and evaluating your children, helping them create novel solutions.

ANALYZE

To begin to analyze the elements of intellect, one needs to know more detailed information about how the brain functions. The brain is a complex organ composed of several interconnected parts with distinct structures and functions that contribute to our cognitive and physiological processes (see Figure 6.1). Here's an overview of some, not all, essential brain parts and their purposes:

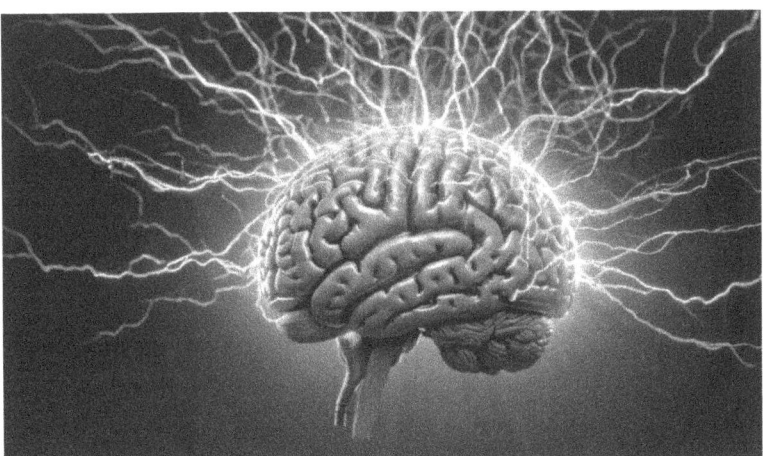

Figure 6.1. Brain

Cerebrum: The most significant part of the brain, the cerebrum, is divided into two hemispheres (left and right) and is responsible for higher cognitive functions such as reasoning, problem-solving, language processing, and conscious thought. It also houses the sensory and motor cortices, which process sensory information and control voluntary movements.

The cerebrum makes us who we are. It represents conscious thought—the things we do purposefully. Conscious thought involves deliberate awareness and control of our mental processes. In contrast, subconscious thought refers to automatic, underlying processes that occur outside of our conscious awareness but that still influence our behavior and perceptions. For example, we might consciously decide to write a book. However, we may put off writing that book for a long time because our subconscious mind, influenced by past experiences, tells us that we are not a good enough writer to complete an entire book. Both conscious and subconscious thought are essential in shaping our cognition, behavior, and experiences.

If your child has subconscious negative thoughts or actions, as in the example above, try to encourage them to move that feeling back into their conscious thoughts. Focusing on a more positive interpretation will enable a child to make a structural change to their brain so as to restructure their pathways. Before they know it, their subconscious mindset will be positive. However, a child can't just say they want to be positive. They must *be* positive, even if it feels unnatural—eventually, their brain will relent and its physical structure will realign.

Brain stem: Situated at the base of the brain, the brain stem connects the spinal cord to the rest of the brain and regulates essential life-sustaining functions such as breathing, heart rate, blood pressure, and consciousness.

If you want to go old school, look up "Schoolhouse Rock, Nervous System."[6] It is a catchy tune that explains the purpose of the brain stem. No complaints if the song gets stuck in your head.

The brain stem integrates and controls the central, peripheral, and autonomic nervous systems. These systems are so effective that they function autonomously or within microseconds before your conscious mind can react. This system highlights the power and speed of brain function.

Prefrontal Cortex: Situated in the frontal lobe, the prefrontal cortex is involved in executive functions such as decision-making, planning, impulse control, and social behavior. It also plays a role in personality, self-awareness, and working memory.

When you think of higher levels of Bloom's Taxonomy, such as analysis and evaluation, think of the prefrontal cortex. This area is what separates us from all other species. Damage to the prefrontal cortex can have profound effects on cognitive functions, emotional regulation, social behavior, impulse control, and personality, impairing various aspects of an individual's daily functions. When I read the zombie horror book *World War Z*, this is the area of the brain I imagined would be damaged when we became the undead.[7] We would simply revert back to our basic instincts without thought or control.

Amygdala: Located in the temporal lobe, the amygdala processes emotions, particularly fear and other emotional responses. It also plays a role in learning, memory, and social behavior.

One of my favorite stories from teaching involves a young man in sixth grade when I was in Texas. The school counselor had recently presented the parts of the brain to the class in an advisory. Later in the week, I walked down the hallway and found him crying in the corner of the cubby area. I approached him and asked him if he was OK and wanted to talk.

He said, "No, Dr. Strecker, I'm fine. My amygdala is just a little sensitive today." He walked away. I went directly to the school counselor, Mrs. Walters, and thanked her for instructing the children about the brain.

These brain parts work together in intricate networks to regulate various physiological functions, process sensory information, generate thoughts and emotions, and coordinate behavior, ultimately allowing for complex cognitive processes and adaptive environmental responses. In other words, we help children develop the systems they need to interact with the world.

This is more than just a biology lesson. When one knows where things happen in their brains, they can take better control of their behavior and mindset. If a person doesn't like something about themselves, they can choose to change it. You can be the person you need to be to achieve your vision. More importantly, you can help children understand their brains better.

Here are some strategies that allow one to effectively analyze one's brain.

- Meditation improves brain function and metacognition.
- Reducing screen time improves cognitive performance by encouraging an active brain.

- Learning new things can create new connectivity in the brain and prime it for learning in the future.
- Applying what you have learned in physical development—eating well, exercising, and sleeping well—can improve your brain structure and function.
- Finally, be careful when using drugs and alcohol. They chemically interrupt your brain processes.

EVALUATE

I'm not asking you to rush out and register yourself or your child for an IQ test. Instead, I encourage you to think about the children you interact with and how they can become the best versions of themselves intellectually. I've included space below for you to jot down your thoughts.

Here are some primers:

What intellectual topics must be understood in your situation to help children find success?

What areas of the brain should I focus on to enhance a child's opportunity for success (memory, processing speed, attention . . .)?

Have they gained full control over their brains, meaning have they mastered the art of bringing to bear logical control over their emotional responses of fight, flight, and freeze?

_____

_____

_____

_____

_____

_____

_____

_____

CREATE

I began this chapter with an Albert Einstein quote. His intellectual journey is a fascinating tale of curiosity, innovation, and groundbreaking insights that transformed our understanding of physics and the universe. He is regularly celebrated as having been one of the most intelligent people on the planet; however, there were times in his life you would not have thought so. Luckily for humanity, he not only committed himself to growing his intellect; he used his entire understanding of the learning process to reach the peak of intellectual achievement. I feel he represents a perfect example of intellectual creation.

Born on March 14, 1879, in Ulm, in the German Empire, Einstein showed an early aptitude for mathematics and science. Despite some challenges in his early education—he often found himself at odds with the rigid educational system—his passion for learning persisted.

In 1905, while working as a patent examiner in Bern, Switzerland, Einstein created and published four groundbreaking papers that would change the course of modern physics. This "Annus Mirabilis" (Miracle Year) included his theories on the photoelectric effect, Brownian motion, special relativity, and mass-energy equivalence encapsulated in the iconic equation $E = mc^2$.[8] These works challenged long-standing notions about space, time, and matter, propelling him into the spotlight of the scientific community.

His subsequent years were marked by further developments, including the formulation of general relativity in 1915.[9] This theory introduced a new understanding of gravity, proposing that massive objects cause a distortion in space-time, which is felt as gravity. It was famously confirmed during a solar eclipse in 1919, catapulting Einstein to international fame.

Einstein remained deeply engaged with philosophical questions about science and ethics throughout his life. He was an outspoken advocate for civil rights, pacifism, and education, and he engaged with other intellectuals of his time, including fellow physicists and philosophers. This is important to note, because his intellect crossed over into the other areas of intelligence, the very essence of holistic development.

Think of all you can do to help children fulfill their dreams and aspirations. It might be something new for your family or your school. Regardless of what it is, I know that a person will need to progress through these levels of learning to increase the odds of maximizing their potential.

SUMMARY

- The brain is a multifaceted and ever-evolving organ. Like myself, it is never too late to begin changing one's brain to fit one's desires.
- The deeper the connections we make, the stronger the response. Think positively as you work on self-development or assist a child in accomplishing tasks to foster their optimistic progress.
- Learn the parts of the brain and what they do. Before you know it, when a child struggles, you will best understand how to support them.

CHAPTER SEVEN

SOCIAL DEVELOPMENT

The best way to find yourself is to lose yourself in the service of others.
—GANDHI[1]

A significant part of family and school life revolves around the social interactions that occur daily. From the moment a Valley School child comes down the stairs for breakfast, to the bus ride to school, to being greeted at the front door, to entering homeroom, and throughout the day, until they are tucked into bed, read a book, and close their eyes for a restful sleep, the interactions are continuous. Human communication is our unique gift, allowing us to share all that we know and understand.

Just like physical and intellectual disabilities, social disabilities also exist. We must help our children adapt to extreme introversion, social phobias, and autism spectrum disorder, just as we do with other difficult situations. Let's start there.

LOVE ON THE SPECTRUM

Have you ever seen *Love on the Spectrum*?[2] It's a TV show about young people on the autism spectrum. I began watching the show because my brother, Matt, recommended it. He mentioned it was one of the most pure and wholesome shows he had ever seen. As I am always looking for inspiration, I clicked on Netflix and started the first episode.

My favorite person to watch is Conner. He is intellectual, witty, handsome, and ethically sound but struggles with social connections and emotional understanding.

In my favorite scene in the show, Connor attends a speed dating event with others on the spectrum. He meets different girls in short sequences. A piece of paper in front of him displays each young woman's name. Connor is supposed to turn in his "yes" or "no" paper to schedule possible future dates at the end of the event. However, Connor has the sheet before him and, more importantly, in front of the women as they are interacting.

Eventually, a young girl named Emily walks up and sits across from him. Pleasantries are exchanged. Connor starts asking her questions, albeit unusual ones, especially considering he has just met her.

Connor asks, "Do you have any allergies of any kind?"

Emily scrunches her nose and says, "What an interesting question to ask, um. Why do you ask? Is my nose—?" She then wrinkles her nose thinking there might be something on it.

Connor says, "No, no, no, no, no, I was just wondering if there were any ... any foods you were allergic to."

After some awkward conversation about peanut butter, Connor asks his next question.

"Do you like nature, by any chance?"

Emily responds, "I guess I am more of a city person."

Connor looks directly at Emily, frowns, holds a pen up, makes a point to click it, and marks a big X in the "no" column by Emily's name. Then he writes "not big on nature" in the comment section. Emily's head sinks to her chest. I didn't know whether to laugh or cry at the uncomfortable social situation.

You might think Connor is mean-spirited, but that is not the case at all. After Emily departs, a production team member asks Connor if he is "writing yes or no while they're (the girls) sitting there."

Connor asks, "Am I not supposed to?"

The producer says, "You might want to wait until they leave. They can probably see."

Connor says, "Damn, I knew I would mess that up."

This is what it means to have social deficits. Here is a group of people whose condition makes it incredibly hard to interact with others. Yet, their social drive to connect is so strong that they will bring to bear their other talents to overcome this. They are so focused on learning the social skills that will enable them to connect that they do everything in their power to understand social etiquette, but sometimes only on an intellectual level.

Later in the season, Connor and Emily go out on a date. There is no way to fully describe the interaction in words; you will need to watch the show or, at a minimum, watch the short YouTube clip. However, to give you a taste, Connor gets nervous and upset after attempting to hold hands. He begins to explain to Emily why he lets go of her hand but fumbles his words. You can tell he is struggling. In the most human of ways, Emily places her hand on his shoulder to let him know it is OK. Connor looks at her sincerely and says, "Thank you," in the most thoughtful tone.

My heart melted.

Human connection is complex and awkward for children. They often struggle to develop a fellowship as they move through life. But it is too important to simply state, "They are just shy and quiet." Social interaction allows children to become wiser, gives them people to empathize with, and guides them while learning ethics. As *Love on the Spectrum* has highlighted, something as gentle as holding a hand or a tight hug in a time of need can change a life.

THE SOCIAL DAMAGE DONE BY MODERN TECHNOLOGY

Over the past twenty-five years, I have watched the very nature of social interaction degrade because of modern technology. This has impacted my own relationships moderately, but I've witnessed an even more significant revolution happening in the lives of our schoolchildren. Growing up, social connectedness was based on face-to-face meetings. It relied on one's ability to read facial expressions, understand the tone and tenor of voices, and recognize body language. However, as the pervasiveness of technology has increased, we are losing this type of connection. Relationships, while becoming more plentiful via social media, are also more superficial. When students discuss friendships, they talk less about acquiring deep relationships and more about accumulating "likes" on Instagram.

This reduction in face-to-face interaction inhibits the development of basic socialization skills. As we become less and less able to read emotional expressions accurately, our empathy is diminished. People need genuine human connection—including touch—in order to bond. However, as with physical and intellectual development, our push for convenience through technology diminishes our social aptitude.

And what do we get in return apart from convenience? Besides reduced social skills, we also acquire an unhealthy need to compare ourselves to others. We develop the *fear of missing out* (FOMO) and encounter increased cyberbullying. Before the internet, we used to go home after work or school and decompress with our families, taking part in activities with other people like cooking dinner, playing with our children, and chatting about our day. Occasionally, you would get a call from a friend, but since you only had one phone line, the rule was not to talk too long. Today, children and adults face a world of constant connection through email, social media, text, phone calls, etc. It is a never-ending barrage of superficial interactions. It makes it challenging to recognize authentic social connections or to find time to relax. As a result, we have higher rates of frustration, anxiety, and depression.

As a precautionary measure, I implore you to consider how to increase authentic social skill building and decrease the amount of time your children spend on superficial social interactions. Protect them against the overwhelming madness of being on their social channels 24/7 (see Figure 7.1).

Figure 7.1. Social Madness

WHAT DOES COMMUNITY LOOK LIKE?

As a counter to the social picture I painted above, I want to share an insight I gained from going on an outing with my younger brother, Matt, and his fellow Marine friends. They wanted to go out for a day of fishing on our boat. Of course, I agreed.

Matt has been out of the service for more than fifteen years but still gets together once a year with members of his unit. He rarely discusses his time in the Middle East with me. This reluctance isn't unusual with groups that return from war. They tend to keep their recollections between them and their close circle of friends. But, for a brief moment, I was allowed to share their inner sanctum of camaraderie.

After a night of pizza and a few libations at the Lagoon Saloon Pub in Port Clinton, we all woke up early to head out fishing the following day. It's difficult to break into a firmly established group. So, for the first few hours, I didn't say much. I simply watched the social interactions. I'm so glad I remained silent. There is something special about observing how members of an intimate group get along, especially those who have laid their lives on the line for one another. They were close and had a friendship that can only be experienced by those who have gone through a similar level of heightened emotion and stress. After returning from fishing, we all gathered around our firepit.

There wasn't some kumbaya moment that day. They hugged when they first saw each other, but their conversation quickly devolved into insults and jokes. They all knew how to exploit each other's weak point, the raw nerve to press on. The ribbing was relentless; I waited for someone to get upset, but the moment never happened. Instead, something unique materialized. They all smiled and laughed, even the victims of the insults. I discovered that it wasn't about the banter; it was about reliving a memory the group members shared that meant they knew one another. The inside jokes formed them into a fellowship. There was a deep underlying trust. The jokes were ways of saying, "You are my brother, and I love you."

My brother, Matt, talks about this type of friendship frequently. He tells people that finding friends is one of the most important things you can do. They are there to lift you up when you desperately need them, even though they spend a lot of time busting your chops. It's all part of belonging to a close-knit group. To let someone into your deepest thoughts and experiences, to show your vulnerability, is truly remarkable. I feel blessed to have joined the group for even a tiny moment.

As you consider your family, friends, and community members, do you share similar trust and love and are you cultivating it in your child? I hope you can say yes.

APPLYING BLOOM'S TAXONOMY TO SOCIAL DEVELOPMENT

REMEMBER

Social development involves multiple components that contribute to your ability to interact effectively with others, form relationships, and participate in society. These components are interconnected and influence each other in complex ways. Here are some critical definitions of social development:

- **Social Skills** encompass a range of abilities that enable you to interact with others effectively.
- **Socialization** is the process through which you learn and internalize the norms, values, beliefs, and behaviors of a society or social group.
- **Relationship Building** with others is a fundamental aspect of nurturing bonds within families, friend groups, and communities.
- **Social Awareness** involves understanding and recognizing the diversity of individuals and communities and the social, cultural, and economic factors that influence people's lives.
- **Social Responsibility** entails actively contributing to the well-being of others and society.
- **Cultural Competence** refers to the ability to interact effectively with people from diverse cultural backgrounds.

Take a moment to consider your family and school. Do you feel the cultural norms and expectations are well understood?

Here is how I try to confirm this at Valley.

Each January at Valley School, I meet with every faculty and staff member to present to them their new contract. After expressing how much I appreciate their individual strengths, which includes authentic feedback, I ask a series of questions.

- Do you feel you have the opportunity to grow at Valley?
- Do you feel emotionally supported?
- Do you feel your physical schedule is appropriate?
- Do you trust your colleagues?
- Finally, how would you describe our community?

The aim is to ensure that the social values emphasized at Valley School are being realized through the perspectives of those interacting with the children.

UNDERSTAND

Social Skills include communication, cooperation, empathy, active listening, conflict resolution, and assertiveness. Developing strong social skills is essential for building healthy relationships and navigating social situations successfully.

Have you heard of MBTI (Myers–Briggs Type Indicator)? As a brief synopsis, if you haven't, introversion and extroversion are personality traits that describe an individual's preferences for social interaction. Introverts enjoy solitude and prefer deep, one-on-one conversations, while extroverts thrive when socializing and being around many others. These preferences influence how you recharge your energy and navigate social situations. Let's add a bit more depth.

Introversion
- They have a preference for quiet environments and internal reflection.
- Introverts feel energized by spending time alone or engaging in solitary activities such as reading, writing, or pursuing hobbies.
- They often prefer deeper, one-on-one conversations over large social gatherings and may find excessive socializing draining.
- Introverts typically process information internally and may need time to reflect before expressing their thoughts or opinions.
- While introverts may enjoy socializing in small groups or with close friends, they prioritize quality over quantity in their relationships.

Extroversion
- They have a preference for social interaction, external stimulation, and outward expression.

- Extroverts tend to feel energized by being around others, engaging in social activities, and participating in group settings.
- They often enjoy meeting new people, attending parties or events, and being the center of attention.
- Extroverts typically think out loud and may prefer discussing ideas or brainstorming in group settings.
- While extroverts thrive in social environments, they may also enjoy solitary activities, but they are more likely to seek out social interaction as a source of energy and stimulation.

Although this seems like an either/or situation, both sets of characteristics are vital for social skill development in children. The only way to maximize their skills in communication, cooperation, empathy, active listening, conflict resolution, and assertiveness is to nurture and apply both introversion and extroversion in various situations. No doubt a child will have an affinity for extroversion or introversion, but be sure to expand on their strengths and improve those things that challenge them.

Socialization begins in early childhood and continues throughout your life, shaping your social identity. Socialization occurs through interactions with family, peers, schools, media, and other social institutions.

Socialization helps you understand the culture in which you live. I am not suggesting you must agree with everything within your culture, for if you accept it unquestioningly, little progress can be made, or worse, you can be brainwashed into biases or prejudices. However, understanding allows you to be attuned to the actions and beliefs of the group you're a part of and then determine whether you want to adopt their values or make changes to your beliefs. This is incredibly important to develop in children. Remember, we teach children how to think, not always what to think.

Relationship Building involves forming connections with family members, friends, peers, colleagues, and other community members. Healthy relationships are characterized by trust, mutual respect, communication, and support.

Listening intently to others is a lost art, but it is essential for effective communication, resolving conflicts, facilitating learning and growth, improving leadership skills, and enhancing personal well-being. Honing this skill in children can cultivate deeper connections with others, foster understanding and empathy, and navigate interpersonal interactions more successfully.

Social Awareness includes recognizing inequality and the needs of marginalized or disadvantaged groups. Social awareness enables you to advocate for social change and contribute to the well-being of society.

You'll remember that we explored the idea of initial conditions in Chapter 4. If you are blessed with some form of privilege in your life (and be careful about claiming you don't have any), using this privilege to contribute to the general welfare of others in society can help them reach a tipping point in their growth. You might offer that extra degree that someone needs to get to their boiling point of success.

Social Responsibility means recognizing your role in the community and taking action to make positive contributions. It may involve volunteering, participating in community service, advocating for social causes, and being environmentally conscious.

I am fortunate to sit as a past president of the Ligonier Rotary Club, an organization with four core elements (see Figure 7.2).

Figure 7.2. Rotary Club's Four-Way Test

The charter aligns well with my own personal values, and I appreciate the group's good work in providing local scholarships, funding community groups, and helping eradicate polio worldwide.

I encourage you to get involved with your Rotary Club or another local organization to be part of something greater than yourself that does good in the world. Remember, your participation directly reflects how others perceive you. Or, as Jason Mraz sings in his song "I'm Yours," "Our name is our virtue."[3]

Cultural Competence involves awareness and knowledge of cultural differences as well as respect for cultural diversity. Cultural competence enables you to navigate cross-cultural interactions sensitively and thoughtfully.

My family did not travel much when I was young. We thought visiting Cedar Point Amusement Park, twenty minutes away from our home, was a long excursion. As such, I didn't have a reference point beyond our tiny little world.

After I got married in college, my wife Stacey and I moved into Ohio State family housing. Stacey and I ran the children's program. To our delight, 95 percent of the students were international. It was the first time I began to expand my knowledge of the diverse cultures of the world, albeit while still in Columbus, Ohio. I certainly would not claim that our experiences were the same as visiting the actual countries, but the families frequently invited us to dinner, and we were able to participate in their traditional events.

I highly recommend putting yourself in situations destined to enhance your understanding of cultures different from your own. They will allow you to become more sensitive and socially adept.

APPLY

> *When we focus on others, our world expands.*
> —DANIEL GOLEMAN[4]

You now have the basic knowledge and understanding of social development to refer to, but to apply these social skills, we must turn to a master and someone I consider a mentor from afar. I first came to Dr. Daniel Goleman's work through his book, *Emotional Intelligence*.[5] We will discuss this more in Chapter 8. I would also highly recommend *Primal Leadership*.[6] Here, I want to discuss his book *Social Intelligence*.[7]

The first question we must answer is, "What is social intelligence?" According to Dr. Goleman, it's a combination of social awareness and social facility.

- **Social Awareness:** Primal empathy, attunement, empathetic accuracy, and social cognition
- **Social Facility:** Synchrony, self-presentation, influence, and concern

Helping children develop these social skills will prove essential to their overall maturation.

Social Awareness

Primal Empathy: In my profession, I frequently have meetings with parents, students, faculty, and staff. Understanding micro expressions on a person's face that are so fleeting they may only last a fraction of a second is vital to communication. What may surprise you is that these are not always picked up in your conscious mind but automatically by your brain's amygdala—its emotional center. You get a feeling, an intuition, about what a person may be feeling or thinking and their intentions. Do not dismiss this instinct. This is your primal empathy at work through mirror neurons.

Mirror neurons were discovered in the early 1990s by Italian neuroscientists led by Giacomo Rizzolatti while conducting experiments with macaque monkeys.[8] They fire when we observe someone else performing an action, "mirroring" the activity in our brain as if we were acting it out ourselves. This process allows us to understand and imitate the actions of others, helping us recognize and empathize with their emotions and intentions.

This is why it is essential when speaking with others to utilize all of your senses. Use your sight to watch a person's facial expressions and body language. Use your ears to listen to the tone and tenor of their reactions. The empathy center in your brain is always running underneath your conscious mind. It is similar to an operating system running code while on a computer. You may not see the emotional 1's and 0's directly but you can feel the results through empathy.

Attunement: Attunement is a concept often used in psychology and interpersonal communication to describe being responsive and sensitive to emotional states, needs, and cues. It involves tuning in to the experiences and perspectives of others and adjusting one's behavior and emotional expression accordingly. In basic terms, it means giving your full attention to another person.

This is incredibly easy to say and much harder to do. If you remember, I talked about focusing on only asking people questions at an event. This is a very useful technique when attempting attunement. The goal is to seek to understand the other person while inhibiting one's desire to add to or refute their opinions. One must listen thoroughly to what they say, how they feel, and what they do. This must be practiced to master, but I am confident when a child does, the other person will likely feel completely understood.

Empathetic Accuracy: Attunement is the process; empathetic accuracy is the outcome. Empathetic accuracy refers to the ability to perceive and understand the thoughts, feelings, and experiences of others accurately. It involves inferring their internal state, such as their emotions, intentions, and perspectives, based on observable cues, and then empathizing with them.

Here are some critical aspects of empathetic accuracy.

Perception of Cues: Empathetic accuracy begins with perceiving social and emotional cues that others convey through verbal and nonverbal communication, such as facial expressions, body language, tone of voice, and verbal content. These cues provide valuable information about the emotional and psychological states of others. Children who develop this skill will likely be elevated in social circles.

As an example, let's say you are speaking with a friend. You ask how they are doing, and they say, "I'm good," but their head is down. The tone of their voice is sad, and they're not smiling. These are your observations based on attunement.

Interpretation and Inference: Once cues are perceived, you must interpret the meaning behind them to understand the thoughts, feelings, and intentions of the other person. This involves making sense of the information available and forming hypotheses about the internal state of the other person.

After taking in the cues from your friend, you begin to make assumptions about their emotional state. They don't seem "good." The vibe you are getting is anything but "good." You make an inference.

Empathetic Response: Empathetic response also entails responding empathically to others based on your understanding, gained through perception and interpretation, of their emotional state. This may involve validating their emotions, offering support and understanding, and demonstrating empathy and compassion in response to their experiences.

You respond with an empathetic tone to your friend. "Are you sure you are OK? You know I am always glad to lend an ear." You step closer and place a hand on their arm, showing compassion.

Accuracy and Error: Empathic accuracy is assessed based on the degree to which one's perceptions and inferences align with the other person's actual thoughts and experiences. While we all want our empathetic accuracy to be high, it can be subject to errors and biases such as misinterpretation of cues or projection of one's own experiences onto others.

Your perceptions of your friend are correct. They are indeed grieving regarding a recent breakup. You sit down and help them begin to process their emotions.

Social Cognition: This plays a fundamental role in human social interaction, communication, and relationships. It enables you to navigate the complexities of the social world, understand the thoughts and feelings of others, and engage in cooperative and adaptive behavior in social situations.

I regularly need to navigate several highly specialized and complex cultural environments, including workplaces, school functions, educational conferences, community gatherings, exclusive clubs, school events, class reunions, family gatherings, and my respite location in Port Clinton, Ohio. I am sure you also shuttle between similarly varied social environments. We know children do this daily. One's ability to be comfortable in all of them speaks to one's skill in social cognition.

As children develop their social cognition skills, they will start to feel less like they are playing a role and more like they are welcomed and appreciated in each environment as their authentic selves. It is important that their core values remain consistent, regardless of the setting. A person must learn to adapt to the nuances of each culture in order to thrive within it.

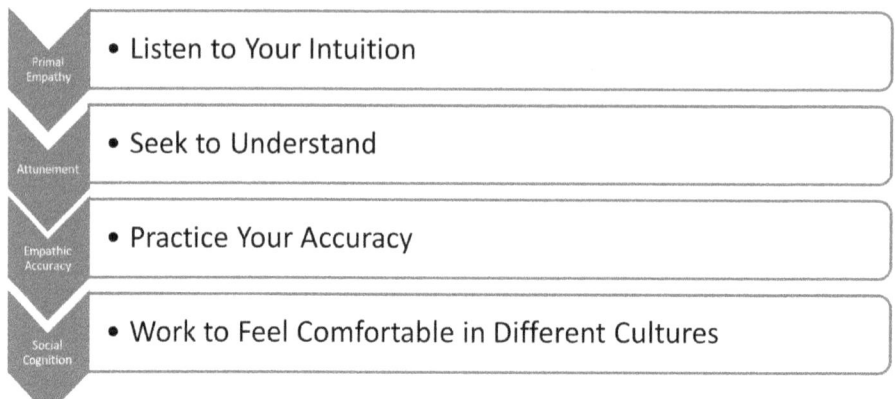

Figure 7.3. The Four Components of Social Awareness

Social Facility

Now let's turn to Goleman's second category of social intelligence: Social facility.

Synchrony: Now that you better understand how your brain connects with others, it is time to use synchrony to connect with another person. You can interact with another person through micro reactions by mirroring facial expressions, tone of voice, and body position, allowing them to connect empathetically. When done correctly, the other person's primal empathy will infer trust and genuine caring; they will feel listened to and completely understood and may even perceive you as highly skilled in the discussion.

I recall navigating a challenging conversation with a parent early in my career. The parent's heightened emotional state and distress for their child were palpable as soon as they entered my office. The parent was seething and accused me of cultivating a group of boys who would put their child in danger.

First, let me explain the circumstances. On a trip to Washington, DC, with an eighth-grade class, a group of four boys had brought a small amount of alcohol on the journey. Three of the four shared the drink. The fourth felt uncomfortable and decided not to participate. Feeling guilty, the boy who didn't participate later told a group of girls. After we returned from the trip, the girls reported it to a teacher, who informed me. As the division head, I called the boys' parents to inform them that I would meet with them on

Monday to determine what happened and what consequences we would levy as a school.

On Monday, the four boys didn't take long to come clean. One child had stowed away a single airplane-sized bottle (50 ml) of Malibu Rum to be shared. Regardless of the bottle size, we wanted to send a decisive message, but one from which the boys could recover.

One by one, I called in the parents. The first three understood the situation and the consequences of their child's actions. The ones with misbehaving students took their child home without complaint. The one who didn't participate returned to class.

As I mentioned above, the fourth parent came into school loaded for bear. She was animated and disparaging. As I watched her intently, she expressed her frustration. I began to nod my head and confirm her feelings when talking about the irresponsibility of the boys bringing alcohol on the trip. Keep in mind that, at this point, she did not think her son participated, because he had told her repeatedly over the weekend that he wasn't involved. Step by step, I mirrored how she sat, her facial expressions, and even her alarming tone at times. The more I did this, the more she calmed down. Before long, once I felt we were in sync, I began to make subtle movements, and she mirrored me, sitting forward and then crossing her legs, for example. Her final question was, "So what will you do to the boys who put my son in jeopardy?"

At that point, I thought she was ready to hear the truth. "I think your son has something to share with you," I said. I invited the young man into my office. She got up immediately and gave him a big momma bear hug.

She put her hands on his face and said, "So what is it, sweetheart?" I invited them to sit and asked her son to tell her what he had told me earlier in the day.

"Mom, I brought the bottle from Dad's stash."

As you can imagine, her demeanor changed immediately. She was thoroughly embarrassed.

We can learn two things from this encounter.

1. The syncing process works. After we synced, I was able to help the mother move into a better state of mind. I was trying to calm her down, not for my sake or the school's sake, but rather so she would be in a

better state to hear what had really happened and then constructively educate her son.
2. When you are a parent, always be careful not to criticize another person or an institution. It may very well be your child who is in the wrong.

Self-Presentation: This refers to the process by which you actively shape and control the impressions you convey to others about yourself. It involves managing your behavior, appearance, and communication to create a desired image aligned with your values and social identity.

As part of this process, one must first identify their core values and who they are as a person. This is why it is so important to instill core values in your children and students. As I mentioned in the section on social cognition, children will navigate varied and complex cultural environments. They should never compromise their goals, values, or identity to fit in.

For me, these values remain intact when I move between various social situations in my life, from our local Fort Ligonier Cannon Ball to the Islands in Lake Erie. For children, they need to understand they will be pressured to conform not only to the expected traditions of the establishment but also potentially to the unhealthy biases and prejudices they encounter.

Influence: A large part of impacting outcomes when interacting with others is the influence you have in resolving conflict. You learn this at a very young age. If you have brothers and sisters, the amount of influence you have in your interactions can be difficult to quantify since you are often presented as sibling equals. However, when the parent of a child walks into the room, they exert a higher level of influence.

When I was young, my two younger brothers, Matt and Mark, tormented me to no end—it was a natural part of sibling rivalry. As brothers do, I would eventually get mad enough to bop, thunk, or push them, although I always stopped short of punching. My father's influence early on ensured I was never violent with my younger siblings.

Influence can be wielded constructively when you have developed a level of social cachet. If you are perceived to offer a level of expertise in a particular area, that respected attribute will cause others to listen to you, thereby exerting influence over the situation. The secret is, as we discussed in Chapter 3, that influence should be wielded with the correct amount of control and autonomy.

Influence can be used in a variety of ways—intellectually, socially, emotionally, ethically, and physically. The more you work toward developing yourself, the more influence you will obtain, all for the right reasons.

Concern: Social concern is a combination of empathy and the will to act. Imagine if someone was crying for help in your home. Would you instantly react, offering your help? The answer is probably yes, because it is a known location and you know the individual. However, as we increase the number of people in any given situation and your familiarity with the person and place declines, you might be less likely to react. Here are some examples:

- You are swimming in your backyard with a friend who is unable to stay afloat and appears to be drowning. Do you act?
- You are swimming in a hotel pool and a stranger appears to be drowning. Do you act?
- You are swimming in a public pool with a lifeguard, and your friend appears to be drowning. Do you act?
- You are swimming in a public pool with a lifeguard, and a stranger appears to be drowning. Do you act?
- You are swimming on a large and busy beach with a lifeguard, and your friend appears to be drowning. Do you act?
- You are swimming on a large, busy beach with a lifeguard, and a stranger appears to be drowning. Do you act?

If you said yes to all six examples, you are one of the rare individuals who shows a heightened level of social concern in all situations. Not reacting to these situations can be for various reasons, including a lack of empathy, not wanting to get involved, panic, or thinking someone else will do it. Whatever the reason, to achieve exceptionalism in social intelligence, you must try to help where reasonably possible.

ANALYZE

With physical and intellectual development, I asked you to analyze yourself. So far, we've only looked at social development through the same lens, but now we will begin to analyze greater society. Knowing this information will help you make micro changes in society that could result in macro impacts. First, let's consider the broken windows theory.

Defined in 1982 by social scientists James Wilson and George Kelling, and drawing on earlier research by Stanford University psychologist Philip Zimbardo, this theory argues that no matter how rich or poor a neighborhood, one broken window would soon lead to many more windows being broken: "One unrepaired broken window is a signal that no one cares, and so breaking more windows costs nothing."[9] Even a small amount of disorder increases fear levels among citizens, leads them to withdraw from the community, and decreases participation in informal social control.

By combining the broken windows theory with the chaos and order theory, you can construct a framework that allows for substantial order while enabling a system's autonomy to evolve. When you apply it to your vision and core values, you will begin to focus on micro details that will lead to macro benefits.

Let's use an example. In our school, we were having a bit of a clutter problem. There were papers on the floor and in the cubbies, causing a mess. The situation had gotten progressively worse over time. The faculty asked me to address the issue with the students. Rather than threatening the children with consequences, I chose to mix the two theories above to explain what happens when we let things become chaotic.

I waited until we all gathered at our weekly meeting in the auditorium. First, I asked the children to look at the room and then close their eyes.

I said, "I want you to imagine a pristine auditorium. Not a speck of dust to be found or a thing out of place; everything perfectly in order." I let them sit in that moment for about ten seconds.

Then, I said, "Imagine one of your classmates walking in and throwing a crumpled-up piece of paper onto the floor." You could see the visceral reaction on the kindergarteners' faces; noses all crunched together to show their disdain.

"Would you pick it up?" I asked. Across all grade levels, everyone nodded and opened their eyes. I then asked one of the fourth graders to explain why.

"Because it shouldn't be there, it makes our perfect environment dirty," she replied.

"How does that piece of paper make you feel?" I asked.

Not even waiting to be called on, an eighth grader said, "Awful and disgusted."

I smiled. "OK," I said, "How about after that, another student walks in and drops another piece of paper, and after that, another one, and so on? Does each piece of paper make you feel better or worse?"

As expected, the children recognized the first piece was the most impactful. Subsequently, the chaos of the paper would become the new norm for the room if unaddressed.

As a collective, we all agreed to try to pick up that first piece of paper to stem the tide of the chaos. And it worked, for a while. Frequent messages are also essential when dealing with elementary school children.

Now, consider a cautionary tale and a reminder. The broken window theory suggests a solution that is meant to add order to a system. However, that solution can be twisted and abused. Some early implementers of the theory were looking for perfect order, meaning they introduced overly harsh consequences for offenders. Instead of inspiring society, it nurtured a fear response. As we've discussed, too much order creates stagnation; too much chaos creates instability. I advise adding order to your systems, inspired by the broken windows theory, but remembering to accept small, incremental changes that show progress rather than taking a zero-tolerance approach.

EVALUATE

Evaluating your families and schools takes practice and commitment. You should see these groups as a fellowship. Once you've established this network, consider the following ways of interacting with your children and students. The fellowship will support you, so the members deserve your support and strength first. This requires you, as a parent and teacher, to be empathetic, attuned, accurate, and masterful in social situations. You must master your ability to sync with others, make a good impression, increase your influence, and show concern for your fellowship. In return, your children and students, as they learn these social skills, will return this support.

I suggest you read back through the application section and think about how you will use these strategies in your homes and schools.

A warning: As you begin to use these social strategies, people will begin to come to you more often for advice, especially the children in your care.

Social Awareness
- Primal Empathy—Are you able to watch and identify the nuanced expressions on people's faces and their body language, allowing your mirror neurons to fire?
- Attunement—Do you give your full attention to the other person while stifling your need to respond?
- Empathetic Accuracy—Are you successful in reading the emotions of others?
- Social Cognition—Do you have the ability to adapt based on social cues and cooperate with others utilizing this social information?

Social Facility
- Synchrony—Do you watch the other person to determine if they are responding to your social cues?
- Self-Presentation—Do you preserve your values as you navigate your varied environments?
- Influence—Have you earned the influence necessary to be seen as a social mentor?
- Concern—Have you developed your empathy and paired that with a will to act so that you can help a person in distress?

CREATE

No matter the vision, one can create something beautiful in this world. Let's look to one of the virtuosos of social change, Dr. Martin Luther King Jr.

Dr. Martin Luther King Jr. changed the world in a profound way as a leader of the American civil rights movement. He passionately advocated for racial equality and civil rights for all, using his powerful oratory skills to draw attention to the injustices faced by African Americans. Dr. King believed in the power of nonviolent resistance, organizing peaceful protests to challenge segregation and systemic racism.

His efforts, alongside countless others in the civil rights movement, led to significant legislative victories, including the Civil Rights Act of 1964 and the Voting Rights Act of 1965.[10] These laws abolished racial segregation in public facilities and protected the voting rights of African Americans. Dr. King's message of equality, justice, and nonviolence inspired millions worldwide and mobilized a diverse coalition of individuals and organizations committed to ending racial discrimination.

Beyond racial equality, Dr. King also advocated for economic justice. He spoke out against poverty and militarism and emphasized solidarity among all people. His vision and legacy continue to inspire generations of activists and leaders. His memory symbolizes hope, courage, and determination in the ongoing struggle for equality and justice. Dr. Martin Luther King Jr.'s contributions have left an indelible mark on the world, significantly advanced the cause of civil rights, and inspired positive global social change.

Dr. King remains one of my social mentors on how to bring about positive, peaceful change in this world. He is a true hero in the most incredible sense of the word.

Your children, too, can exert social influence for good if they take the time to master the social levels of learning. It will start with influencing a single person, move to their family and friends, eventually to their workplace or school, then to their town, and quite possibly the world.

SUMMARY
- Watch out for nefarious influences, such as modern technology and social media, that detract from your authentic social experience and development. Seek out authentic social connections that are based on face-to-face interactions.
- Get your children involved in your local community to develop their social skills, help them build a fellowship, and contribute to the social environments they take part in.
- Look to the work of Goleman when developing your social intelligence in children, focusing on social awareness and social facility.
- Work toward improving their social awareness, including their primal empathy, attunement, empathetic accuracy, and social cognition.
- Work toward improving their social facility, including their synchrony, self-presentation, influence, and concern.
- Teach them to show concern for others in all situations as a way to extend their community connections.
- Remember the broken window theory and what it tells us about the impact of catching the first thing that introduces chaos into the system.

CHAPTER EIGHT

EMOTIONAL DEVELOPMENT

Never speak out of anger, Never act out of fear, Never choose from impatience, But wait ... and peace will appear.
—Guy Finley[1]

Let's start with an example of unadulterated emotional dysfunction. This situation represents underdeveloped emotional regulation in its purest form. I hope you do not experience this level of rage in your family or schools, although I recognize it does happen.

CHICAGO ROAD RAGE

My wife and I visited her sister in Chicago a few years ago. Two cars pulled up alongside us as we were driving home on Lakeshore Drive down by Navy Pier. The first car, a Ford Explorer, had cut off a Chevy truck in thick traffic. The driver of the Chevy laid on his horn and made a well-known hand gesture. For the next mile, the two drivers engaged in aggressive driving, swerving in and out of traffic next to each other. My wife begged me to back away, which I did, but I stayed close enough to watch the chaos unfold.

At one point, the traffic bottlenecked. The Chevy pulled up beside the Ford, and the two drivers exchanged verbal threats, pointing and cursing at one another. The situation was beginning to escalate from a regular confrontation into serious road rage. The traffic started to move. The Ford driver leaned out his window, threw a cup of liquid onto the front windshield of the Chevy, and drove off. The Chevy driver turned on his windshield wipers and tore after the Ford. Once again, the traffic slowed. The Chevy caught up to the Ford and pulled up alongside. As the guy in the Ford was leaning out his window and continuing to engage, the driver of the Chevy threw what I can only assume was a vanilla milkshake into the open Ford window. It exploded throughout his car.

As the traffic started to move again, the rivals exited the highway onto a side street. In my last glimpse of the action, I noticed the two men in a standoff. One man was holding a tire iron, and the other was reaching under his shirt for something—a weapon, I can only assume. I don't know what happened, but I was dumbfounded by how things had escalated to such emotional chaos. To avoid potentially dangerous situations, it is critical to master the skill of emotional regulation in yourself and your children.

EMOTIONS—A PRIMAL FORCE

Emotions can be considered a primal force within human beings. They're deeply rooted in our evolutionary history, playing a crucial role in the adaptation and survival of our species over thousands of years.

Emotions are powerful triggers that help us respond to different stimuli in our environment. For instance, fear activates a "fight, flight, or freeze" response, preparing us to confront a threat, escape danger, or remain still until the threat passes. This instinctual reaction was crucial for early humans when facing predators or other dangers in the wild. However, in modern times, these responses can still be triggered even when we no longer need such protection. These negative emotional responses often inhibit our ability to find successful solutions.

In contrast, positive emotions like joy and compassion promote prosocial behaviors and bolster collaboration and mutual support—all essential for social bonding, our well-being, and the survival and flourishing of social groups. These emotional reactions support the other intelligences, reinforcing their positive attributes.

While our modern lives may seem far removed from the primal challenges of our ancestors, our emotional responses remain profoundly ingrained and continue to shape our thoughts, behavior, and decision-making processes. They influence everything from personal relationships to societal dynamics and political movements. Indeed, they still guide us toward choices designed to maximize our chances of survival. For instance, desire and attraction motivate us to seek out potential partners, while disgust helps us avoid potentially harmful or contaminated substances.

However, they can be an albatross around our necks too. Remember what I said about chaos and order? As the opening example demonstrated, uncontrolled emotions promote unhealthy levels of turmoil and pose significant dangers in both personal and professional spheres. When left unchecked, emotions can lead you to make irrational choices on impulse. Some of these choices may result in you feeling regret. More importantly, uncontrolled emotions can strain relationships with colleagues and friends.

Also, from a health perspective, chronic stress resulting from unmanaged emotions can affect your physical well-being and weaken your immune system. Persistent emotional havoc may contribute to depression or anxiety.

If one grapples with unmanaged emotions, they are likely prone to engaging in self-sabotaging behaviors or withdrawing from social interactions. This can lead to isolation and more emotional pain. Identifying and managing emotions effectively is crucial for navigating life's challenges and building healthy relationships.

And our emotions do not affect only us. They impact those around us. As the opening example showed, they can spread from person to person just like a virus. And the damage caused is based on the virulence of the strain—the level of anger or sadness. We can spread positive emotions, too, and this is something we can do with intentionality to lift those around us (see Figure 8.1).

Figure 8.1. Emotional Contagion

In this phenomenon, called emotional contagion, people "catch" the emotions of others, either consciously or unconsciously, through mimicking, mirroring, or internalizing those emotions. It's driven by the tendency for individuals to synchronize their emotions with others around them, often without even realizing it.

Emotional contagion can occur in various social settings, including face-to-face interactions, group settings, and even through indirect means such as social media. For example, if someone in a group expresses joy or enthusiasm, others in the group will likely start to feel happier or more upbeat, even if they were not initially feeling that way.

People are more likely to catch the emotions of others when they feel empathetic toward them, when they perceive a solid emotional connection, or when they consider them to be authority figures. It is, therefore, important to evaluate your fellowship's emotional state.

This is why mastering the skill of emotional development carries so much weight for you as a parent or teacher. People you know will be responsive to your emotional demeanor, resulting in a more substantial influence. Take a moment to consider your emotional disposition as a family or school. Is it one of positive or negative morale, hope or pessimism, or enjoyment or displeasure? Children are highly susceptible to cultural emotions and, in many ways, act like little mirrors. What we give out is often reflected to us.

Each morning, I greet the children at the front of the school, aiming to ensure that their first interaction of the day is filled with positivity and happiness. I do this through a series of high-fives, fist bumps, and handshakes. My personal favorite moment is with one student, where we celebrate the days of the week: Monday, Pre-Hump Day, Hump Day, Friday Eve, and the all-glorious Friday. This tradition has been going on since this child was in kindergarten (he is now in eighth grade). This ritual would be much less effective if it were not matched by the enthusiasm and positive spirit of the faculty and staff. But it is, every day, in every classroom, in the dining hall, in the athletic facility, at recess, in music, and so on. While it may seem surreal, all indicators from faculty and staff surveys, parent surveys, and student feedback show high levels of trust and satisfaction.

We often think of contagion as negative, but truth be told, positive contagion is much more influential.

THE EMOTIONAL DAMAGE DONE BY MODERN TECHNOLOGY

Social media platforms can profoundly impact our emotions, influencing how we interact with others in both positive and negative ways.

On the positive side, social media provides opportunities for connection and self-expression. It allows us to stay in touch with friends and family, regardless of geographical distance. It can lead to a sense of belonging and community, even if it cannot replace in-person interaction.

However, the impact of social media on our emotions is not always positive. Excessive use of social media has been linked to feelings of envy, particularly when comparing oneself to others' highly curated and often idealized representations of their lives, which I mentioned earlier in the book.

Cyberbullying and online harassment are prevalent on social media platforms, causing significant distress for victims. The constant barrage of hate is a disturbing by-product of impersonal contact. Emboldened by "keyboard courage," people will say the most despicable things online when they are hidden from view and not there to see the other person's reaction.

The addictive nature of social media can also impact our emotions. The constant notifications, likes, and comments we experience when posting or following others' posts can trigger a release of dopamine in the brain, creating a cycle of validation seeking that can be difficult to break. This can lead to feelings of anxiety or stress when we are unable to access social media or when our posts do not receive the desired level of attention.

I worry for this next generation. With the decline in physical health, intellectual capacity, authentic social connectedness, and ever-increasing emotional issues, you have to wonder if the convenience of technological breakthroughs genuinely outweighs the negative impacts.

The Annie E. Casey Foundation works to develop a brighter future for children and youth at risk of poor educational, economic, social, and health outcomes. Here are some of their key findings on social media and teen mental health in their blog (posted August 2023 and updated June 2024):

- Studies show that with increased levels of social media among children and adolescents, these adverse effects are prominent: "Depression and anxiety, inadequate sleep, low self-esteem, poor body image, eating disorder behavior, and online harassment."

- "Nearly 2 in 3 adolescents are 'often' or 'sometimes' exposed to hate-based content on social media."
- "Studies have found a connection between social media cyberbullying and depression among young people."
- "Teen girls and LGBTQ youth are more likely to experience cyberbullying and online harassment, which can lead to negative emotions."[2]

The Casey Foundation also highlighted these negative impacts on teens:

- They miss out on real-world friendship and socialization opportunities.
- They become highly self-critical (often due to comparing themselves to false realities presented on social media).
- They experience cyberbullying.
- They feel increased levels of stress and isolation.
- They struggle to concentrate at school or at work.
- They fail to sleep soundly or get a good night's rest.
- They stop practicing positive self-care and self-reflection.[3]

As an educational professional, these findings give me pause. I believe technology can still be used sparingly as a tool to meet people. However, we have to begin to moderate its use and intentionally teach children, at a young age, the dangers it poses to our emotional health and the value of holistic development.

As an example, a parent once asked me when it would be appropriate to get a child a cell phone. I responded with a line I had heard from another head of school: "When you want their childhood to be over." A sobering but accurate statement on the impact of technology.

APPLYING BLOOM'S TAXONOMY TO EMOTIONAL DEVELOPMENT

REMEMBER

Daniel Goleman's impact on the field of emotional intelligence (EI) is profound. His book, *Emotional Intelligence: Why It Can Matter More than IQ*, brought the concept to prominence and emphasized its crucial role in our success.[4] His work has influenced psychology, education, leadership, and organizational development, and has inspired training programs to improve emotional skills, especially in schools and businesses. Indeed, Goleman's advocacy has led to global recognition of EI as essential for personal and professional growth.

But what is emotional intelligence? It refers to a set of abilities that enable you to recognize, express, and manage your own emotions as well as perceive and respond to the feelings of others. These skills, sometimes known as emotional competencies, are essential for navigating the complexities of interpersonal relationships.

Here are some critical emotional skills:

Self-Awareness: The ability to recognize and understand one's emotions, including triggers, strengths, weaknesses, and values.
Self-Regulation: The capacity to manage and regulate our emotions in a healthy and constructive way.
Empathy: The ability to understand and share the feelings and perspectives of others.
Social Awareness: The skill of accurately perceiving and understanding the emotions and social dynamics of groups in various situations.
Emotional Expression: The capacity to express emotions openly and authentically without resorting to suppression or avoidance.
Emotional Resilience: The ability to bounce back from setbacks, challenges, and adversity.
Optimism: The tendency to maintain a positive outlook and perspective even in adversity.

These emotional skills are interrelated and complementary.

UNDERSTAND

Let's put these terms into context.

Self-Awareness: Self-aware individuals are in tune with their feelings and can accurately assess how their emotions influence their thoughts and behavior.

Have you ever sat and thought about how or why you feel a certain way? As one deepens their understanding of their own emotions and becomes familiar with their triggers, one will begin to act intentionally in situations rather than impulsively in reaction to their feelings. They may also begin to carefully choose when and where to engage in conversations. Now, imagine mastering this skill in yourself and then reflecting the impact you can have on a distraught child. Rather than being emotionally reactive as they hurl an insult at you, you take a breath and begin to discover the underlying cause of their emotions.

Self-Regulation: Self-regulation means controlling your impulses, managing stress effectively, and adapting to changing circumstances without becoming overwhelmed by strong emotions.

One of the most important times to consider one's feelings is after a hard day at school or work. Before walking into the house, a person should make themselves aware of how they feel. If feelings are negative, they should ask their family or friends to give them a moment to decompress alone or sit with them and process what they're going through—this is part of the regulation process. They should find a quiet place and recharge. This way, when they engage, those around them won't be receiving the pent-up emotions they "caught" from elsewhere.

Empathy: When empathetic, a person is sensitive to the emotions of others, can accurately perceive their needs and concerns, and can respond with compassion and understanding.

After mastering one's emotions through self-awareness and regulation, they are ready to help others. By practicing listening thoughtfully to others and reading between the lines to perceive their feelings, a person will know why they say what they say.

Remember that listening to someone with high emotions can directly impact one's own emotions. They are riding a roller coaster with many ups and downs. Make sure not to get in the car with them, but remain at the controls, keeping a level of emotional distance and objectivity.

Social Awareness: When socially aware, one will be adept at reading nonverbal cues, understanding social norms, and navigating interpersonal relationships effectively.

Give your full attention to others, maintain eye contact, listen to their tone, and watch their body language. These will all help a person study and discern these nonverbal signals. This also requires one to shut off the TV, put their phone down, and take out their ear buds. Be present!

Emotional Expression: Skills in emotional expression allow a person to articulate your feelings constructively, promoting self-understanding and fostering genuine connections with others. The power of this ability cannot be overestimated.

I like to think my optimistic outlook on life makes a difference at Valley School. Whether it be at chapel, at after-school dismissal, or passing students in the hallways, I try to express my belief that life is a blessing and every day is meant to be cherished and not wasted.

On occasion, however, I encounter a student who instantly makes a positive emotional impact with nothing more than a smile—it is a natural gift in some. Each morning, a particular young lady walks in with a huge smile on her face. She has a wide-open grin with a few missing teeth that can only be interpreted as pure joy. The conversations among the others become more upbeat and optimistic when she greets them. Her emotional expression makes a great impression.

Emotional Resilience: Once emotionally resilient, a person can cope with stress, disappointment, and failure effectively, using setbacks as opportunities for growth and learning rather than becoming overwhelmed by negative emotions.

We all face ups and downs, tough times, regrets, and mistakes. A child's life is filled with them. Their ability to recover from these events is a sign of strong emotional intelligence.

Optimism: If a person is optimistic, they find hope and meaning in difficult situations, which enables them to persevere and maintain motivation toward their goals.

This might be the most impactful characteristic of emotional intelligence. Hope provides a spark of light in the darkness of despair. That light often separates failure from success.

Let's look at another benefit of optimism. I consider myself a highly optimistic individual. I mean, I have survived two life-altering health scares, have a wonderful family, and have an incredible career working with an uplifting faculty and staff, students, and families. I feel completely fulfilled in life. Needless to say, it is easy for me to remain positive.

During a particularly tough spell for a group of students, I needed to redirect them to get them back on track. I promised myself I would remain measured when addressing them, but when the time came, I was visibly firm when I expressed my disappointment. I never raised my voice, but I am sure the children had never heard me talk that sternly to them.

About a week later, I had a parent tell me a story. They said their child mentioned that Dr. Strecker addressed the class and he was really frustrated. Because it was rare, and I was known to them as a positive and optimistic person, the parent and the child's older brother, who graduated the year before, said, "You made Dr. Strecker mad? He is never mad. You guys must have really screwed up."

Because I was seen as a positive and optimistic person, this feedback had a greater impact on the children, and the outcome was more productive. They listened to me. In comparison, if you are always pessimistic, yelling at your child or students at every opportunity, that becomes your baseline, and people begin to ignore your message.

Another way to understand your emotions is the ability to accurately name them in yourself and others. To do this, you must acquire a profound vocabulary (see the emotions wheel in Figure 8.2).

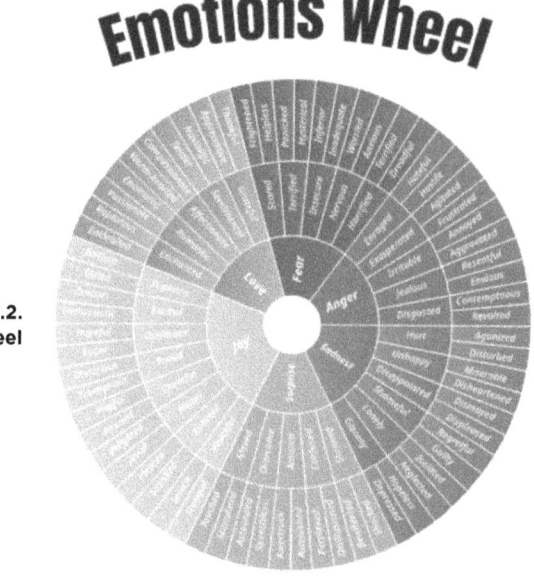

**Figure 8.2.
Emotions Wheel**

I recommend you print this off and keep it close at hand. As one experiences more emotions and cross-references them with the wheel, adding the words to one's vocabulary, a person will become increasingly skilled at identifying one's feelings accurately and the feelings of others.

Speaking in public, for many people, is one of the scariest things to do. I still get nervous walking up to a podium to deliver a message. When I first started speaking in public, fear was the only appropriate description of my emotions.

However, it turns out I'd mislabeled my emotions. *Webster's Dictionary* defines *fear* as "an unpleasant, often strong emotion caused by anticipation or awareness of danger."[5] Speaking in public is a safe situation. It may be humiliating, embarrassing, or demoralizing, but it's not dangerous. After looking more deeply at the vocabulary of emotions, I realized I was, more accurately, *anxious*. *Webster's Dictionary* defines *anxiety* as "characterized by extreme uneasiness of mind."[6]

From that point forward, knowing what emotions I was dealing with, I was better able to prepare myself for the uneasiness of my mind. I used a variety of coping skills I had developed over the years to overcome my trepidation. I convinced myself that the pre-speech feelings were actually a combination of anxiousness and excitement. My brain was preparing me to unleash the necessary emotion to deliver an inspiring speech. The nervousness has never gone away, but the excitement now supersedes it.

Speech advice: Include intentional pauses in your speeches. This gives you a moment of reflection, allowing you to choose your words carefully. It ensures clarity and precision in communication and reduces the likelihood of misunderstandings or misinterpretations. This helps reduce feelings of anxiety, increases confidence, and emphasizes key points, making your speech more impactful.

You can also use pauses in conversations, allowing you to regulate your feelings and respond thoughtfully rather than reacting impulsively in heated moments. It encourages active listening as it creates space for others to contribute to the conversation and promotes a more collaborative, respectful, and calm exchange of ideas.

APPLY

In the graphic below (Figure 8.3), we can see the journey we take when we develop a new skill or gain new awareness—moving from unconscious

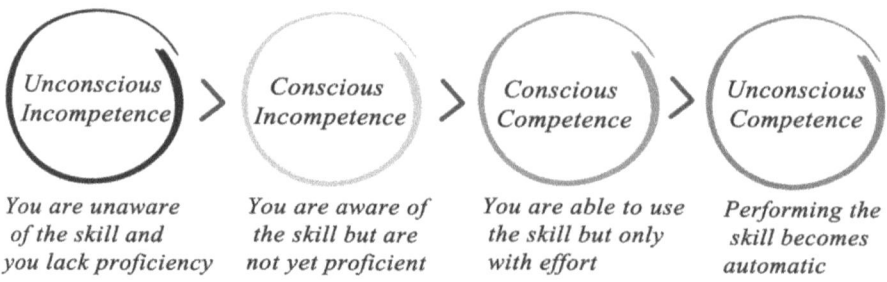

Figure 8.3. Unconscious Incompetence to Unconscious Competence

incompetence to unconscious competence. It is a bit awkward to say these terms, but once I explain each level, it will be easy to comprehend.

You just have to remember the difference between subconscious and conscious learning. Once you understand it, you will look at your child's or student's learning sequence with incredible clarity. Let's use the example of learning to play an instrument.

Imagine you're embarking on learning a new skill: playing the guitar. At the outset, you're in a state of *unconscious incompetence*. You don't even realize what you're missing; the guitar seems mystical, and you're oblivious to the depth of skill required to master it. You may have seen others play and admired their ability, but the closest you've come to playing is "air guitar," or the video game *Rock Band*.[7]

Then comes a moment of realization: *conscious incompetence*. Perhaps you pick up a guitar for the first time and strum a few strings only to realize how difficult it is to produce a clear sound, let alone play a melody. You become aware of how much practice you will need to undertake with the guitar to enhance your skills. It's a humbling moment, but it sparks your desire to learn.

You begin your journey of deliberate practice and learning. You take lessons, watch tutorials, and diligently practice chords and scales. In this *conscious competence* phase, you're fully engaged in the process. Every strum and every chord change require concentration. You play some songs, and you're making progress, but it's slow and deliberate. You're aware of what you're doing, but it takes a lot of effort, and you're actively working to improve.

As time goes on and you continue to practice, something remarkable happens. You enter the realm of *unconscious competence*. Playing the guitar starts to feel natural, almost effortless. Your fingers move instinctively across the fretboard, finding the right chords without conscious thought. You lose yourself in the music, and it flows from you freely. You've reached a level of mastery where the skill has become a part of you.

You have transitioned from ignorance to mastery, from unconscious incompetence to unconscious competence. It's a testament of will to wisdom and a reminder that we can achieve exceptionalism in any skill when we apply ourselves with dedication and effort.

Well, guess what? That same concept applies to all developmental skill building. Let's take emotional intelligence as an example. Our early years are spent grabbing, slapping, and crying when we don't get our way. We experience our own emotions but don't understand that others have them as well. This is an example of *unconscious incompetence* when it comes to empathy. You don't know what you don't know.

Time passes, and our families teach us that others have feelings too. You might be asked, "How would you feel if someone took your toy?" At some point, you begin to understand that others have emotions, but you are not good at comprehending them—*conscious incompetence*.

After years of effort and practice, you understand emotions intellectually, socially, emotionally, ethically, and physically. You recognize how your mirror neurons pick up on other people's subtle facial gestures, tone, and body language, and you purposefully watch for these telltale signs. This stage is called *conscious competence*.

Finally, you find yourself sitting across from others without thinking about how to react to their emotions. Still, you always seem to help the other person feel understood and say the right thing at the right moment. People begin to ask you for help to solve their emotional issues. This ability comes to you without any effort. Your *unconscious competence* has been activated. You have reached the level of subconscious mastery. Helping others emotionally comes as easily as riding a bike.

This four-part sequence works for all five developmental areas. However, I chose to introduce it in relation to emotional development because emotional skill building is difficult and incredibly valuable. We often find it taxing when we deal with someone else's emotions and they can elicit emotions within us. You can become an asset to any person, school, or community if you can effectively manage your feelings and help others manage theirs. Once you have mastered this skill, your children and students will be the ultimate beneficiaries.

ANALYZE

Although emotional mastery can make the world a better place when it's used with positive intentions, it can also be used against a person. It's important to be aware of how and why it might be used for nefarious means and watch out for common tactics.

Some people will use emotional manipulation and persuasion to exploit deep-seated emotions and vulnerabilities, such as fear, insecurity, and the need for acceptance. These tactics can be wielded with precision and subtlety, making them difficult to detect. For instance, manipulators may employ charm to gain trust as they promise to fulfill one's desires. They may also shower a person with affection—often known as "love bombing"—before gradually exerting control over them. These are common tactics of narcissists.

In addition to exploiting emotions, manipulators may leverage psychological tactics to maintain dominance and control. This can include intermittent reinforcement, where rewards or punishments are delivered inconsistently, creating confusion and dependency. They may also employ gaslighting techniques to sow doubt in one's mind as to their recollection of events and distort their interpretation of reality, making them more susceptible to manipulation.

In romantic relationships, for example, an emotionally manipulative partner may use tactics like withholding affection to maintain power and control. In the workplace, manipulative leaders may use charisma to maintain authority and suppress dissent.

Sometimes, it is difficult to tell the difference between positive and nefarious intentions because someone's intent defines whether it's manipulation.

Let me give you an example. Let's go back to Cedar Point Amusement Park in Sandusky, Ohio. I was coming off my first spring term at Ohio State and was excited to return to my hometown area to work and perhaps find a girlfriend. They placed me in Kiddieland. Being a single guy, I liked my odds. The female/male ratio in the department was seven to one. I was fond of a brunette named Stacey. I must have asked her out ten times before realizing she saw me as a friend rather than a romantic interest—the dreaded friend zone. Regardless, we still spent a lot of time together.

Each morning before work, we would gather under the overhang and chat. I noticed she would quite often be a bit aggravated. I later learned the most appropriate word would be "hangry," a combination of angry and hungry. Without thinking much about it, I began bringing her a little breakfast. As the summer progressed, we grew closer. Finally, she asked me why I always got her food.

I said, "Well, when you eat, you are happy. When you are happy, you smile. And you have a beautiful smile." Guess what? I got my first date, and we are still married thirty years later.

There is a reason I bring this up as part of our manipulation section. I was telling a group of bright middle school math students the story. When I finished, one of the boys laughed and said that I had *Ivan Pavlov*-ed her. Pavlov, a Russian physiologist, observed that dogs naturally salivated at the sight of food. By consistently pairing a neutral stimulus (such as the ringing of a bell) with the arrival of food, he found that those dogs began to salivate in response to the bell alone.[8] They formed an association between the bell and food, known as classical conditioning. I was the bell, you see.

I explained my honest intent to the students. Regardless, the math students referred to me as Lord Strecker, Master Manipulator, for the rest of the year. One boy even made some business cards with that name emblazoned on the front. My point is that some people may have had malicious intent in this situation, and that is what defines manipulation. As a person masters emotional intelligence, they will begin to pick up on this type of emotional inauthenticity and safeguard themselves against it.

In today's world, this skill is more important than ever for our children to learn. It seems that manipulative behavior is on the rise, using virtual social-emotional tricks to pull them in.

EVALUATE

I was fortunate to begin my university education experience focused on psychology. The combination of learning introductory psychology, neuropsychology, and biopsychology had a pivotal impact on my maturation and enabled me to better evaluate my own emotional intelligence. Here are some strategies to help a person evaluate their EI by assessing their emotional skills and competencies:

> **Undertake a Self-Assessment:** Consider how you typically respond to stress, conflict, and challenges. Pay attention to self-awareness, self-regulation, empathy, and social skills.

- **Seek Feedback from Others:** Seek feedback from trusted friends, family members, colleagues, or mentors about emotional intelligence. Ask them to provide honest insights about how one interacts with them, handles emotions, and communicates effectively. Their perspectives can offer valuable insights into one's EI strengths and areas for improvement.
- **Try Journaling:** Keep a journal to track emotions and behaviors over time. Write about experiences, including how one feels, why one might feel that way, and how one responds. Reflecting on journal entries can help one gain insights into patterns and areas for growth.
- **Observe Your Interactions:** Pay attention to interactions with others in various situations, such as at school, in social settings, or with family members. Observe how one communicates, listens, and responds to others' emotions. Notice patterns in behavior and consider how one can improve one's emotional skills in different contexts.
- **Use Professional Development Opportunities:** Seek opportunities for professional development in emotional intelligence. Attend workshops or courses on developing emotional skills such as self-awareness, empathy, communication, and conflict resolution. Role-playing, reading case studies, and group discussions can enhance one's understanding and application of emotional intelligence concepts.

By using a combination of these strategies, a person can make steady improvements. Once you feel skilled, begin applying these skills to your children and your students. Even if it is a free moment at the end of class, a short lesson may provide that spark that makes a difference.

CREATE

Eleanor Roosevelt was a trailblazing figure in American history, known for her remarkable advocacy and commitment to social justice. She embodied the principles of empathy and compassion. Born into privilege in 1884, Eleanor faced challenges early in life, including the loss of her parents and a complicated relationship with her mother-in-law, Sara Delano Roosevelt. However, she emerged as a resilient and compassionate leader, reshaping the role of First Lady during her husband Franklin D. Roosevelt's presidency.

Eleanor used her position as First Lady to advocate for the rights of marginalized groups, including women, African Americans, workers, and children. She held press conferences, wrote a syndicated newspaper column, and traveled extensively across the country, engaging with citizens and giving voice to their concerns. Eleanor's advocacy played a crucial role in advancing vital social reforms, such as establishing the National Youth Administration and adopting the Universal Declaration of Human Rights by the United Nations.

Beyond her domestic work, Eleanor was also a prominent figure on the world stage. As a delegate to the UN General Assembly, she was pivotal in drafting the Universal Declaration of Human Rights. This landmark document affirmed the inherent dignity and rights of all individuals. Her efforts earned her widespread acclaim and recognition, leading President Harry S. Truman to declare her the "First Lady of the World."[9]

Throughout her life, Eleanor demonstrated her high emotional intelligence and her ability to utilize these skills for good. Despite facing personal hardships and public scrutiny, she remained steadfast in her commitment to justice and equality. Eleanor Roosevelt's life is a testament to the transformative power of applying the elements of *Emergence*.

SUMMARY

- Emotions are a primal force that has evolved to help us survive threats. However, in the modern context, uncontrolled emotion causes conflict and stress, particularly when it's exacerbated by technologies such as social media.
- We must work from unconscious incompetence to unconscious competence in our development of emotional intelligence.
- Emotional intelligence involves competencies such as self-awareness and social awareness, self-regulation, empathy, resilience, emotional expression, and optimism.
- It's useful to increase your emotional vocabulary to remain as precise as possible when defining and expressing emotions.
- Watch out for emotional manipulators. Emotional intelligence can also be used for nefarious means.

CHAPTER NINE

ETHICAL DEVELOPMENT

Live your life as though your every act were to become a universal law.
—KANT[1]

According to *Webster's Dictionary*, *ethics* is "A set of moral principles: a theory or system of moral values or the principles of conduct governing an individual or a group."[2]

Of all the types of intelligence, ethical intelligence might be the most challenging to define and agree upon. While many individuals can reach a consensus on the significance of intellectual, social, emotional, and physical intelligence, ethical intelligence is heavily influenced by specific cultures and religious beliefs. Therefore, I will explore ethical intelligence through a philosophical lens; however, I encourage you to consider the ethical elements present within your own families and schools.

For context, Valley School is a nonsectarian institution. We respect the observance of all religious beliefs but do not promote any singular ideology. In our view, ethics are defined by integrity, morality, humility, and mindful interactions.

Let's begin with the importance of ethical decisions and their impact on a person.

JURY DUTY: AN ETHICAL ROLLER COASTER

Sitting on a jury is one of the most challenging places to practice ethics. I have been selected three times to serve on a jury. Two of the cases were monetary: a car crash and a business dispute, so the ethical issues involved were relatively minor. The third, on the other hand, was a physical assault case. Sitting on a jury and testing your ethics profoundly impacts you for a long time. Having to decide on the guilt or innocence of a person is draining. All your emotions, and those of your fellow jurors, come out.

It is essential to give you a bit of background when discussing the ethical dilemma we faced as a jury. A man physically assaulted a woman in her home. During the assault, she picked up the phone and dialed 911. She threw the phone under the bed, and the entire audio interaction was recorded. The police arrived and arrested the man for physical abuse.

During the trial, we were presented with evidence, including pictures of the home, torn clothing, and the phone audio. At this point in the trial, I was relatively confident in my ethical assumptions, but things became more complex later when three pieces of evidence came to light.

1. We discovered they had been boyfriend and girlfriend for a year. This does not change the fact that it was abuse, but some jurors considered the information critical.
2. The woman who had been assaulted took the stand and said she was not attacked and that she didn't want to press charges. This also impacted the jury. However, in Indiana, once an assault case is established, it is no longer the victim's decision as to whether to press charges; it is up to the state. The state proceeded with the case.
3. The assault victim, while on the stand, let the jury know she was pregnant and that she didn't want her boyfriend to go to jail because he paid the bills.

Once the arguments in court were finished, we moved into deliberations. Even though I was much younger than most of the jurors, they asked me to be the foreman as I was an administrator, and they thought I seemed fair. I have learned a couple of ethical truths since sitting on a jury. First, people are highly reactionary to emotionally charged events, so it is not wise to leave your fate to a jury of your peers. Second, people are typically led by their dominant trait when they make their arguments, whether that's physical, intellectual, social, emotional, or ethical intelligence.

- Emotional Development—Those who were emotionally intelligent discussed the emotions of the woman and man as the event happened.

They also sympathized with the woman and her plight of losing a financial resource.
- Physical Development—Those with physical intelligence discussed the physical damage to the woman.
- Social Development—Those with social intelligence discussed the impact on society if we ruled guilty or innocent and felt this was more significant than what happened to them as individuals.
- Intellectual Development—Those with intellectual intelligence focused on defining physical assault and whether the facts met the criteria.
- Ethical Development—Those with ethical intelligence looked closely at whether the man's actions were right or wrong.

We knew our decision had to be unanimous before we told the judge we were ready. So, we sat and discussed for many hours. Things became heated, so I decided to call for an anonymous vote. With twelve jurors, we had five guilty, five innocent, and one undecided. I abstained because I wanted to remain impartial as the foreman. Everything was intensely debated. I was even called "the devil" at one point because I wouldn't openly agree with another juror's viewpoint. I took my job of remaining impartial seriously.

After three more hours of debate, we decided the man was guilty. However, I remain convinced the verdict would have changed if there had been additional developments—perhaps the child's birth. It was hard not to be swayed by the woman's plea. Without a doubt, we all felt terrible for her regardless of the outcome.

Anyone who says that ethics is easy misses the point of being human. Ethics is an essential part of our lives, without which we have no scale of right and wrong. However, defining right or wrong is a very difficult and often subjective thing. I mean, to one woman, I was Lucifer himself. I am only half joking. Her emotions rose; she was the last holdout for the man's innocence. I think the weight of the moment just got the better of her.

THE WEIGHT OF ETHICAL DECISIONS

Ethical development begins in early childhood and continues throughout one's lifespan. It is influenced by your upbringing, cultural norms, education, and personal experiences. Naturally, as a child, you learn basic moral concepts and social norms through interactions with your peers, parents, and authority figures. Then you begin to distinguish between right and wrong and learn to follow standards of conduct. Here is a short story to reinforce the point.

My wife works in preschools and provides emotional and social support for teachers. She often comes home with humorous stories about the children. One day, she was sitting in a class of three- and four-year-old children, watching them interact. The children were playing nicely when one little girl, Ella, screamed, "Tony just said a bad word." The teacher, who had been working with Ella about falsely tattling on her classmates, looked at my wife questioningly. My wife had not heard a thing, so she shrugged in response. The teacher got up to investigate.

Tony, the boy accused, was a boisterous little guy, so the teacher suspected she would have heard him if he had sworn. The teacher turned to Ella and said, "I'm sorry, Ella, but no one heard Tony say a bad word." Ella stormed away in a huff.

The teacher and my wife both turned their attention to Tony. The boy's eyes squinted as his mouth drew into a smirk, and he proudly said, "That's because I said it *willy, willy* quiet."

You have to love children! In all seriousness, this demonstrates how ethics are learned. Ella was rightly trying to hold her peer to account for doing something she considered unethical, although she was struggling with her own ethical compass, learning to stop fibbing about others. Tony, on the other hand, failed to see his ethical misstep at all, although he was at least honest about what he did.

As you grow and mature, your ethical development becomes more complex, influenced by cognitive, social, and emotional factors. You begin to engage in moral reasoning by considering the consequences of your actions and their impact on others. You develop a sense of integrity, aligning your behavior with ethical beliefs and values (see Figure 9.1).

Imagine you stand at a point where an ethical decision must be made. It could be taking credit for someone's work in school, maximizing your profit by offering a client an inferior product at work, or, as a doctor, ending the life of a terminally ill patient by discontinuing treatment at the patient's request.

Each of us faces difficult choices in life that simultaneously test our intellect, emotions, and morals. In many cases, there is no definitive correct answer. The process involves an internal conflict within our minds. Let's take the example above of a doctor ending the life of a terminally ill patient at their request.

ETHICAL DEVELOPMENT   149

Figure 9.1. Moral Dilemmas

Intellectually, I believe you could rationalize the need to discontinue giving a person medicine if the terminally ill patient requests it. The process of death is a natural one, and something that we will all go through at some point, so allowing it to occur earlier than expected in certain circumstances is not illogical. Similarly, one could make the argument that it is an ethical thing to do as the patient should have control over their own body and decisions regarding their life. Finally, emotionally, we could probably reconcile the act of supporting them if there was no hope for recovery and the person was in immense pain. If you are like me, you might imagine the patient in this scenario is an older person at the end of a beautiful life who wants to pass peacefully.

However, we can slightly vary the context here to make the dilemma more complex. Let's say the patient is nineteen years old and has been diagnosed with cancer. The medicine might, in fact, cure them, with the odds of a cure set at 50/50, but the treatment is excruciating. Without any treatment, the prognosis is only twelve months of life. So, let's weigh the options.

1. The patient may feel pretty good until their death in a year.
2. The patient may experience excruciating treatment for twelve months and then be cured.
3. The patient may experience excruciating treatment for twelve months and then die.

What do you do as a doctor? What do you suggest to the patient? I know most of us would say any chance is better than none, so choice 2, but to experience intense pain for a sustained period is not something we can take lightly.

I encountered a situation like this when I was going through cancer at twenty-one years old. I was at the end of my own treatment and was headed for remission. I was fortunate. My doctor asked me to speak to a young man who was having a difficult time handling the chemotherapy.

He was a nineteen-year-old boy who had been recently diagnosed with stage IV cancer like me. The boy had just gone through his first round of treatments and was not doing well. He had requested that they stop. His parents were encouraging their son to continue, and the doctor was hopeful he would change his mind. But he was an adult and could decide to end his treatment without anyone else's permission.

If you do not have experience with cancer, you may not know how difficult going through chemotherapy is. The reason they use it is because it kills all the fast-growing cells in your body, including the tumor. But it does this while simultaneously killing you. I was once asked to describe it. Have you ever stayed up all night, maybe twenty-four to forty-eight hours straight? Your body starts to feel heavy. It hurts to move. Your joints are inflamed. The desire to sleep is constant. However, no matter how long you sleep, that feeling does not subside. Throw in the fact that many people are incredibly nauseous immediately after treatment and it is a heck of a pill to swallow for an entire year or longer as you receive treatment. I completely understood what this young man was going through.

Of course, I agreed to talk with him. Ultimately, I would like to think he chose to return to treatment, but truth be told, I don't know. I gave him my number in case he wanted to talk, but he never called. The three options I listed above were his way of explaining the situation. That was the way he tried to rationalize his ethical dilemma, by breaking it down into three simple choices. I genuinely hope I run into that young man again someday, and I hope he is well.

TWO PERSPECTIVES ON ETHICS

We might all feel that we understand what ethics are intuitively, but let's consider how it's been defined intellectually. I'd like to look at the work of two of the foremost thinkers on the subject—Immanuel Kant and Bruce Weinstein.

IMMANUEL KANT

Kant (1724–1804) was a German philosopher who is widely regarded as one of the most influential figures in modern philosophy (see Figure 9.2). He made significant contributions to various areas of metaphysics, epistemology, ethics, and political philosophy. Kant's work has profoundly impacted numerous fields of study and continues to be studied and debated by scholars worldwide.

One of Kant's most significant contributions is his ethical theory known as Kantianism. At its core is the notion of the categorical imperative. He defines this as a universal moral principle that applies to all rational beings. Kant argued that moral actions are performed out of a sense of duty, guided by the categorical imperative rather than our personal desires.

Kant expressed the categorical imperative in different ways. First, let's look at his Formula of Universal Law: "Act only according to that maxim whereby you can at the same time will that it should become a universal law."[3]

Figure 9.2. Immanuel Kant

In simpler terms, when considering whether an action is morally right or wrong, you should ask yourself if you would be willing that everyone else act similarly in a related situation. If you can imagine everyone following the same rule or principle without causing contradictions or chaos, then the act may be ethically permissible. However, if allowing everyone to act in the same way would lead to logical inconsistencies or negative consequences, then the action is likely ethically wrong.

For example, perhaps you decide to lie to someone to get out of trouble. Applying the Formula of Universal Law, you would ask yourself whether you want everyone else to lie whenever they are in trouble. If everyone lied in similar situations, trust would break down, communication would become unreliable, and society would suffer. Therefore, according to Kant's formula, lying in this context would be considered morally wrong because it leads to a contradiction when it becomes a universal law.

He also expressed morality in the Formula of Humanity: "Act in such a way that you treat humanity, whether in your person or the person of any other, never merely as a means to an end, but always at the same time as an end."[4]

Again, in simple terms, this means that you should always respect the inherent value and dignity of human beings, both yourself and others. Instead of treating people as mere tools or instruments to achieve your goals or desires, you should recognize and honor their worth as individuals with their own goals and rights.

For example, imagine you are hiring someone for a job. Treating them according to the Formula of Humanity means that you should not simply view them as a means to fill a position or complete tasks, as we did during the Industrial Revolution, but rather as a person with their own talents, dreams, and needs. You should treat them with respect during the hiring process and ensure that the job provides fair compensation and opportunities for growth.

Kant was so committed to this idea that he even postulated that one could be unethical to oneself. Imagine sitting on the couch and mindlessly scrolling through your social media accounts. Kant would argue that in those wasted minutes you are being unethical to yourself as you are not trying to maximize your own potential. You are underappreciating your own value and broader desires as a human being.

While I appreciate Kant's contributions, his philosophies might be a bit myopic for the diverse perspectives of the modern world. However, I think we should appreciate his attempt to develop universal solutions to ethical conundrums.

BRUCE WEINSTEIN

The world has changed so much in the last 150 years that we must consider ethics from a modern perspective, as well. Bruce Weinstein, also known as The Ethics Guy®, is a renowned ethicist, writer, and speaker who emphasizes practical ethical principles for individuals and organizations. He initially caught my eye because he was one of the first ethicists to use the phrase *ethical intelligence*, and he authored a book by the same name.[5] He believes, as I do, that we can develop ethical intelligence just as we can develop intellectual, social, emotional, and physical intelligence.

Let's review Weinstein's core ethical ideas.

Integrity: Weinstein emphasizes the importance of integrity, which involves consistency between one's actions and ethical principles. Acting with integrity means being honest, trustworthy, and adhering to moral values even in challenging situations.

When speaking with children, I emphasize that integrity is essential when people are watching you, but meaningful ethical behavior occurs when no one is watching. You must be consistent with your own morality, even when you know you won't get caught.

When my son was thirteen years old, he and I were checking out at a CVS store. He saw a $100 bill lying on the ground. He picked it up and looked at me. It was a perfect ethical dilemma to learn from.

I asked him, "What should we do?"

He shrugged, not knowing.

I said, "Let's turn it in to see if someone claims it."

We looked at the cashier, an older lady in her sixties, and handed over the bill. Another cashier, a bit younger, likely in his mid-twenties, looked at us quizzically. I assume he was thinking, *Put it in your pocket and run, kid.*

When we got home, my son asked me why we didn't keep it. Rather than tell him, I posed another question.

"How would you have felt if you had put that bill in your pocket?"

My son looked at me and said, "It's not quite like stealing it but also not like earning it."

I am glad my son recognized that finding something that is not yours does not mean you automatically get to keep it. I thought that would be the end of it. However, thirty days later, I got a call from the lovely lady at CVS. She said no one had claimed that $100 bill and we could drive back to the store to pick it up.

Watching my son take the money without guilt was one of the ethical highlights of my life.

Respect: Weinstein advocates for treating others respectfully, regardless of their background, beliefs, or status. Respecting others involves listening attentively, valuing diversity, and recognizing every individual's inherent worth and dignity.

This is a good strategy to balance the initial conditions we discussed earlier. By prioritizing respect for all, we can begin to minimize this world's inherent biases and prejudices. This will take significant effort and time, but may we all strive to achieve unity and hope as a collective.

Responsibility: Weinstein emphasizes taking responsibility for one's actions and decisions. This includes acknowledging mistakes and making amends when harm has been caused. Responsible behavior also involves considering the consequences of one's actions on others and taking proactive steps to minimize damage.

Here's a powerful lesson in accountability that I remember from my childhood. In the 1970s cartoon version of *'Twas the Night Before Christmas*, a young mouse climbs up inside a clock tower to see how it works. Unfortunately, he breaks the clock in the process, eliminating any chance that Santa will visit the town. He confesses. "I didn't mean it, Father; I'm sorry." I'll always remember what Father Mouse tells his son: "It's not enough to be sorry when you have done something wrong; you must correct the thing you did."[6]

To me, that is taking responsibility for one's actions.

Fairness: Weinstein promotes fairness and justice in interactions and decision-making. Fairness entails treating people impartially without favoritism or discrimination. It involves considering the perspectives and interests of all stakeholders and making decisions based on principles of equality.

When I worked in Texas, I had the honor of coaching the John Cooper School sixth grade football team. During our undefeated season, my son played on the team. My son's physical intelligence was reserved for music, not football, however. Each day, he would take the field, and every fiber of my being wanted him to play. It didn't help that my wife was yelling from the stands, "Put Strecker in!"

However, being fair and equitable, I couldn't put him in without showing favoritism. I had to choose players based purely on ability in order to properly carry out my role. In the end, it all worked out. My son just graduated from Penn State University with a degree in the arts.

Compassion: Weinstein underscores the importance of compassion and empathy in ethical behavior. Compassion involves understanding and empathizing with the experiences and feelings of others and acting with kindness and concern for their well-being.

These characteristics should already be a focus of your children's development, given all you have learned about emotional and social intelligence. However, the difference between knowing what to do and deciding to do it is ethical intelligence.

THE DAMAGE DONE BY MODERN TECHNOLOGY

The digital landscape and social media profoundly influence ethical considerations in modern society. They pose challenges and opportunities that reshape how individuals navigate ethical dilemmas. Here are some recent sobering statistics relating to modern technology and the ethical issues they raise:

- According to a study by the Pew Research Center, about 64 percent of Americans believe that fake news causes a great deal of confusion about the basic facts of current events.[7] This highlights the ethical responsibility of social media platforms to manage misinformation. A survey from the Knight Foundation found that 68 percent of Americans believe social media companies have a moral obligation to combat misinformation.[8] This statistic highlights the expectations of users for ethical conduct from platform providers.

- A report from the Data Protection Commission revealed that over 80 million data breach records were reported on social media platforms in 2021 alone.[9] This raises ethical concerns related to user privacy and data protection.
- A survey conducted by the Federal Trade Commission indicated that only 60 percent of influencers disclose their relationships with brands.[10] This raises ethical questions about transparency and authenticity in influencer marketing.
- Research published in the *Journal of Politics* found that social media users are more likely to be exposed to partisan content, with an alarming 90 percent of social media news feeds containing information that aligns with users' existing beliefs.[11] This suggests that social media use has serious implications for balanced ethical discourse.
- A report from the Royal Society for Public Health in the UK found that over 70 percent of young people said that Instagram has a negative impact on their mental health.[12] This raises ethical concerns about the content promoted on social media platforms and their impacts on user well-being.
- The Cyberbullying Research Center reported that approximately 36 percent of young people between ages twelve and seventeen have experienced cyberbullying.[13] This statistic points to the ethical obligation of social media platforms to create safer environments for their users.

These statistics suggest that social media enables harmful behavior that directly undermines Kant's and Weinstein's ethical principles. A large part of teaching ethics is understanding the consequences of abusing the societal values that allow us to move forward positively. The anonymity and social distance provided by social media platforms can encourage individuals to ignore their moral obligations, as they know there are few consequences. The truth is, we are better able to grasp these consequences and hold to our moral obligations when we look people in the eye, see their facial expressions, and read their body language.

Likewise, social media's role in spreading disinformation is incredibly harmful. The rapid spread of fake news challenges ethical principles such as integrity and the responsibility to verify information before sharing it. This undermines trust in the media, ultimately impacting societal norms.

We must master ethical intelligence to cultivate a more moral digital world. Promoting ethical behavior on social media requires transparency and respect for others' rights and well-being, despite anonymity. Fostering a digital environment that upholds ethical principles and promotes positive social interactions is imperative.

ETHICS IN SOCIETY

These trends have fostered an erosion in trust. Certainly, media and politics are two areas where this is true, and I will highlight them further in this section, but I want to start with how students today have been influenced to misrepresent the truth to push their own agendas. Unfortunately, the degradation of our moral standards is hitting home.

A student was not doing well in a math class. Upset by his grade, he was looking to punish the teacher for holding him accountable. Using an online picture of the teacher and some AI technology, he created a profile using the teacher's name and pictures. The student then posted a handful of radical posts that he knew would inflame the public. It worked. The teacher was called in and questioned. After the teacher explained that he didn't even have a Facebook account, the school managed to locate the guilty student and applied significant discipline. However, the teacher's reputation was already tainted, and trust was eroded. Deepfakes are becoming ever more common in modern society.

If you have been following societal research, you will be familiar with the erosion of trust in two of our most critical societal structures: the media and the government. These two arenas have undergone seismic shifts in recent years.

Media Trust: In the past, traditional media outlets, such as newspapers and television networks, were often regarded as trusted sources of information, playing a crucial role in shaping public opinion and discourse.

Now, however, trust has been eroded to a frightening extent. The rise of digital media and social networking platforms as news providers has led to more bias, sensationalism, and misinformation in reporting. They also encourage more polarization in our views rather than a search for the more nuanced truth. We see the media as being less ethical and we therefore do not trust what they tell us.

Political Trust: Historically, democratic societies have relied on trust in government institutions, elected officials, and political processes to ensure legitimacy and social cohesion. This has dropped significantly in recent years, fueled by narcissism, bellicose behavior, and corruption scandals on both sides of the aisle, which destabilize our society. With foreign countries trying to manipulate our elections, we lose our belief in our system.

Distrust in political institutions has led to apathy and disengagement from the process. It doesn't seem that a day goes by without a scandalous story appearing.

I think it is safe to say that in America, and elsewhere, this is only getting worse. It has begun to affect our schools and families. Without correction and the reestablishment of ethical standards, the worst of humanity may very well become commonplace.

So, how can we change this worrying trend? By building ethical networks. But what are these?

We need to foster communities and nurture individuals dedicated to moral principles. By promoting trust and credibility at the local level, ethical networks can create a foundation that will shape social norms, influence attitudes, and ensure positive behaviors within our communities.

Despite the unethical behavior of our leadership, news outlets, and many social media communities, we must turn the tide. The only way to accomplish this is by individually inspiring each other with our own ethical behavior.

When you think of your friends, family, schools, and communities, do they reflect and promote an acceptable level of ethics? If not, what can you do to create change?

APPLYING BLOOM'S TAXONOMY TO ETHICAL DEVELOPMENT

REMEMBER

Let's begin shaping your expertise on ethical intelligence. Here are the moral elements you want to consider:

- **Integrity:** Integrity involves ensuring consistency between your actions and ethical principles. It entails honesty and adherence to moral values, even when facing challenges or the temptation to compromise them.
- **Respect:** Respect for others' dignity, autonomy, and rights is fundamental to ethical conduct. It involves valuing diversity, listening attentively to others, and treating them with fairness.

Responsibility: Ethical behavior entails taking responsibility for your actions and their consequences. You must acknowledge your mistakes, learn from your failures, and make amends when harm has been caused.

Fairness: Fairness and justice are core principles of ethics. Fairness involves treating people equitably and without favoritism or discrimination, ensuring that decisions are made based on the principles of justice.

Compassion: Compassion involves having empathy for others' suffering and reacting with kindness. It's about understanding and acknowledging the experiences and feelings of others and acting with generosity.

Trustworthiness: Trustworthiness is built on honesty, reliability, and consistency in behavior. It involves being dependable and worthy of trust and confidence.

Empathy: Empathy involves understanding and sharing your feelings and perspectives. It enables you to connect with others on a deeper level, fostering awareness and mutual respect.

UNDERSTAND

Understanding these ethical principles and skills is essential for developing healthy friendships, family relationships, and community bonds. It's also the foundation for healthy self-development. Let's look at how to better grasp the complexity of ethics.

It's subjective and complex: Ethics involves navigating complex and often subjective moral dilemmas. What is considered ethical can vary widely depending on cultural, religious, and personal beliefs. Understanding ethics requires acknowledging this complexity and being open to diverse perspectives.

As the world becomes more connected, we will increasingly experience the overlap of contrasting and contradictory ethical standards. This exposure will hopefully lead us to a universal standard of ethics, but I am afraid we will experience more conflict before we can find a resolution. Just know that these varied opinions will lead to complex situations. This makes it that much more critical to enhance your ethical dexterity.

It's guided by principles and values: Ethics is guided by principles and values that shape our moral reasoning, decision-making, and behavior.

Some elements of ethics are irrefutable. Honesty, fairness, and respect represent our north stars and are worthy of our understanding. I recommend a person create an individual pledge to hold these characteristics in the highest regard.

We must consider both intentions and consequences: Ethical evaluation often involves considering the consequences of actions as well as the motivations and values that drive people's behavior. Understanding the interplay between intentions and impact helps a person assess the ethical implications more comprehensively.

When someone says something hurtful to another, emotions are raised, and the resulting conversation can often dissolve into a shouting match. Instead, we should seek to understand what is behind their words and offer grace if the hurt was unintentional. The offender must then focus on why their words were hurtful and attempt to learn from it.

It involves continual learning and reflection: Ethics is not a static concept but an ongoing process of learning and growth. Ethical understanding evolves as you engage with diverse perspectives and reflect on each other's values and beliefs.

The old adage that the most intelligent people know that they know nothing holds true here. It is time for us to take a humble approach rather than a win-at-all-costs attitude. I see far too many online personalities condescendingly seeking out a fight in order to win a debate. Equally, I see far too many activists who have shut down well-intentioned speakers for a cause they believe in. Mastering ethics is discovering what you don't know, not just reinforcing what you do.

Ethics must be applied to real-world situations: Ethics isn't just about theoretical scenarios. It's about applying your moral principles and values to real-world situations. It involves developing the capacity to analyze ethical dilemmas and act according to one's ethical convictions. It requires practical wisdom and a commitment to moral action.

This topic transitions nicely into the application portion of ethical development. The theoretical world allows us to explore ideas freely and without consequence, but the real world forces us to feel the burdens of our moral actions. I encourage you to practice in the theoretical realm to hone your skills before applying them in reality.

ETHICAL DEVELOPMENT   161

APPLY

As I stated earlier, it is wise to practice ethical development using theoretical scenarios. The more you practice, the more you will see how people justify their ethics based on how they process information. In principle, in any situation, there are a multitude of different ethical choices that can be made and just as many justifications that can be proposed. Let's consider a hypothetical case.

The Trolley Problem (see Figure 9.3) is a classic ethical dilemma often used in moral philosophy to explore moral reasoning and decision-making. It presents a scenario where a runaway trolley is heading down a track toward four people who are tied up and unable to move. They will be killed if the trolley stays on its current path. You are standing next to a lever that can divert the trolley onto another track where only one person is in peril. Do you pull the lever, sacrificing one person to save four, or do you refrain from acting and allow the trolley to continue its course, resulting in the deaths of four people?

The Trolley Problem raises profound ethical questions, exploring the principles of utilitarianism, which emphasizes maximizing overall happiness

Figure 9.3. Trolley Problem

or minimizing harm, and deontology, which prioritizes adherence to moral rules or principles.

In utilitarianism, pulling the lever to divert the trolley is seen as the morally preferable choice because it minimizes harm and serves the greater good by saving the lives of four people at the expense of one.

On the other hand, from a deontological perspective, some argue that pulling the lever violates the moral principle of not directly causing harm to others, even if it results in a greater overall good. Hence, you would not pull the lever.

The Trolley Problem illustrates the tension between these two ethical frameworks and the complexities of moral decision-making. It challenges you to consider the ethical principles at stake, weigh competing moral obligations, and grapple with real-life ethical dilemmas' inherent ambiguity. It's a thought-provoking tool for exploring moral reasoning and the foundations of ethical theories.

So, which choice would you make? Do you pull the lever or not? What if the single person was your mother? This is why the ethics of good and evil are overused. I hear it far too often to explain situations and events. I believe in the existence of good and evil, but I reserve such words for the direst of situations.

ANALYZE

Let's analyze an ethical dilemma commonly encountered in healthcare settings and focus on solid analysis techniques to make a decision.

Scenario: A physician working in a resource-constrained hospital must decide how to allocate a limited supply of life-saving medication. Several patients in critical condition require the medication to survive, but there are only enough doses available to treat a fraction of them. The physician must decide which patients will receive the medication, knowing that those who do not receive it will likely die. Note that this isn't such a far-fetched scenario. During the height of the COVID-19 pandemic, there were shortages of ventilators in hospitals, and doctors had to make similar decisions.

Ethical Considerations

Justice: The principle of justice requires fair and equitable distribution of resources. The physician must consider factors such as medical need, prognosis, and likelihood of benefiting from the medication when deciding how to allocate it among patients. Avoiding discrimination or favoritism is crucial in upholding the principle of justice.

Beneficence: The principle of beneficence emphasizes the obligation to act in patients' best interests and promote their well-being. The physician must prioritize patients' health outcomes and strive to maximize the overall benefit of the available medication. This may involve prioritizing patients with the greatest likelihood of survival or those in the most critical condition.

Autonomy: Upholding patient autonomy requires involving patients in decision-making and respecting their preferences and values. However, in this scenario, patients may be unable to participate in decision-making due to their critical condition.

Nonmaleficence: The principle of nonmaleficence dictates that healthcare providers must avoid causing harm to patients. In this scenario, the physician faces the ethical dilemma of potentially withholding life-saving treatment from some patients, which may result in damage or death.

Transparency and Accountability: The physician must ensure transparency in decision-making and be accountable for their decisions.

In resolving this ethical dilemma, the physician may engage in a collaborative decision-making process involving a team to develop an allocation process based on ethical principles and clinical considerations. The physician may also seek guidance from hospital policies. Ultimately, the goal is to make decisions that prioritize patient welfare, uphold principles of justice and fairness, and mitigate harm to the greatest extent possible.

So, what decision would you make? You can understand why I want to sit this one out. It's a nightmare. If you are a sci-fi fan, you will remember when James T. Kirk had to participate in the Kobayashi Maru experiment in an episode of *Star Trek II: The Wrath of Khan*.[14] It was a simulated rescue mission involving a distress call from a civilian vessel that was stranded in the Neutral Zone. The scenario presented challenges that made it impossible to rescue the ship without violating Starfleet regulations or risking the crew's safety.

It is an unwinnable situation.

I hope for your sake that you are not presented with ethical dilemmas such as these. But if you are, I hope you can forgive yourself.

EVALUATE

Evaluating oneself ethically involves a deep and ongoing process of reflection and self-awareness. Here's how you can approach it with your children and students.

- Recommend setting aside time for quiet reflection. Consider recent situations they were involved in or decisions they had to make where ethical considerations were at play. Help them investigate their motivations and consider the consequences of their actions from an ethical perspective. Evaluate whether their decisions resulted in positive or negative outcomes for themself and others in the short and long term.
- Clarify their personal values and ethical principles. Think about what matters most to them in terms of honesty, integrity, fairness, compassion, and respect for others. Consider whether their actions align with these values and whether there are any discrepancies.
- Have them seek feedback from trusted friends, family members, or mentors. Ask them for an honest assessment of how they feel about their actions and whether they believe they're acting ethically. Encourage them to be open to constructive criticism and use it as an opportunity for growth.
- Learn from any ethical mistakes they've made in the past. Reflect on what led to these lapses and how they can avoid similar situations in the future.
- Finally, act on their insights and commitments. Actively integrate ethical principles into their daily life and decision-making.

By thinking of ethics as a process, something they can work on and that will evolve, they will see it in much the same way as they view physical, emotional, intellectual, and social growth.

CREATE

Up to this point, I have given you famous people to admire and emulate. In this chapter, I would like to highlight my mother, Margaret Strecker. Being raised by the right person is vital to one's ethical development. Life is an incredible journey, one filled with mentors and misery makers. In my life, my mother represents the most underappreciated hero I know.

Despite our large family (there were seven of us) and the fact that there was not enough money to go around, we managed. Between Monday and Thursday, my wonderful mother worked all day but always had time to show us love and treat us fairly and respectfully. One way she met our physiological needs was by taking an enormous pot and making a huge helping of one of the four delicacies (chili, spaghetti, mac and cheese, and goulash). That meal lasted us many times over until Thursday because, if not, it was back to bologna sandwiches and bananas. Of course, by the time Thursday rolled around, we were so sick of the "magic pot of unending sustenance" that we would scoop out the remains and feed it to our highly overweight Basset Hound named Brownie. "Chili nights" were an olfactory nightmare.

However, every Friday, our wonderful mother made homemade pizza, and we all got together for movie night. The laughter, the smiles, and the close connection she nurtured impressed upon me the importance of family and societal happiness. So it went, week after week, shuttling from Monday through Thursday survival to weekend glory. Occasionally, I would sneak to my friend's house for burgers and dogs. My legendary five hamburgers-in-one-sitting nights still live on in the tales of Greenwood Heights and Union Street lore.

Regardless of our unfortunate financial position, my mother was a master mentor in emotional stability and ethical fortitude. All five of us chose professions in service to others. My sisters Angie and Heather became nurses, I became a teacher, and my brothers served our country in the Marine Corps. The mantra she instilled of doing the right thing in difficult situations was foundational to our upbringing.

I hope my story shows you how important committing to ethical growth is to one's maturation. The power you have when you develop yourself can be everlasting. Think about the impact you can have on yourself, your family, your students, and your community. The only way we change this world is by one person at a time. Despite our current declines, you can reverse the trend by making lasting changes from within.

SUMMARY
- Ethical behavior involves integrity, respect, responsibility, fairness, compassion, trustworthiness, and empathy.
- To understand the foundations of ethics, study the great philosophers.
- Use ethical theory to contemplate ethical dilemmas.
- Never feed your dog chili. Whoa!

CHAPTER TEN

COMPLEXITY OF DEVELOPMENT

The Interrelation of the Five Intelligences

The whole is greater than the sum of its parts.
—ARISTOTLE, 322 BCE[1]

I have previously presented the five intelligences of self-development in singular, mostly disconnected forms. This approach was important for understanding how to help a child master each element individually. However, we are now on the brink of a significant realization. Using these five intelligences in isolation does not reflect complexity in its most influential form, one of true exceptionalism. Let's begin with a definition.

Webster's Dictionary defines *complex* as "a whole made up of complicated or interrelated parts."[2]

A child is a whole being, and as the definition implies, they are made up of complex and interrelated developmental parts. It is not enough that they master these five intelligences alone. Rather, they must combine them in sophisticated ways to maximize their full potential so they can emerge as their fully transcendent self. This is not a metaphysical concept but rather the result of enhancing and ultimately mastering intellectual, social, emotional, ethical, and physical intelligence.

Emergence, then, is the culmination by which these five intelligences are combined simultaneously.

EMERGENCE: A PATH TO TRANSCENDENCE

In *Emergence*, my intent was to ensure that you understood the concept of mastering the five intelligences through the levels of the Bloom Taxonomy—Remembering, Understanding, Applying, Analyzing, Evaluating, and Creating. If a child is to achieve these steps, eventually they will be able to bring something unique and novel to the world—true transcendence.

Let's consider the pathway to transcendence based on my former professor's work—Dr. Timothy Jones.

Dr. Jones, in his article titled "Complexity Theory," highlights three areas of the self-organization of living things; self-maintaining, self-renewing, and self-transcending.[3]

Self-maintaining refers to the intrinsic ability of a system to uphold its functionality and existence without external interference. This concept is observable in both biological organisms and technological systems, where mechanisms are in place to regulate internal processes and sustain operations autonomously.

Since I mentioned *World War Z* earlier in the book, let's use an apocalyptic reference to explain these three levels of complexity. Let's imagine that we had to start over as a species, so to speak. The first level we would need to ensure is self-maintaining our existence. At a minimum, we would need to create a structure that provided us with the basic elements, according to Maslow, in regard to physiological and safety needs. Our water, food, shelter, sleep, and clothing become pivotal. A system that would allow for these needs would be defined as self-maintaining. Survival would be assured.

There is nothing wrong with this if you are satisfied with simplicity. If you have enough food to eat, a safe place to rest your head, and the basic resources to get by, then you can survive. However, you might have to travel for food and seek out suitable environments to prosper.

Self-renewing denotes the capacity of a system to regenerate or replenish itself, ensuring its longevity and adaptability. This concept is exemplified in biological systems through processes like cellular regeneration and tissue repair and in technology through automatic updates that enhance performance and extend lifespan.

In the self-renewing scenario, the people would need to create a functional biosphere that consistently resupplied them with all the elements they required for survival. In terms of physiological needs, they would need to have a freshwater source nearby, enough wildlife for food, and a permanent shelter that would safeguard them from the elements.

Self-renewing individuals tend to meet life's needs by working to provide for their families. In exchange for their efforts, they are paid money. With those funds, they purchase the resources they need to survive. They are self-reliant but have limited time for upper-level complexity.

You should begin to see the connection between these three levels with the evolution of the human species over time. I feel comfortable in stating that we have mostly fulfilled these two levels of development in our cultural maturation. As a matter of point, I believe we were headed toward self-transcendence until recently.

Self-transcending is about surpassing our current limitations and striving for higher complexity, understanding, or capability levels. In philosophical and personal development contexts, self-transcendence involves growth beyond one's current state of being. Similarly, in technology, self-transcending systems evolve beyond their original design or purpose, acquiring new functionalities through ongoing development and innovation.

Let's imagine we could start over knowing everything we know now. We first met the basic needs of individuals—physiological and safety needs (general welfare). We sustain those needs permanently using self-renewing systems such as farming, water purification, and basic housing, allowing for elements of love and belonging (domestic tranquility). However, to truly manifest the blessings of liberty, we must transcend beyond our current limitations. I believe this can be the true power of *Emergence*.

Self-transcendent people are different. They not only take pride in having met their basic needs and finding a way to ensure their needs are met permanently; they also want to ensure everyone's needs are met fully, so they can continue to transcend. If a person were inclined to meet this lofty life challenge, they would bring to bear Einstein's intelligence, Martin Luther King's social impact, Tony Horton's physical health, Eleanor Roosevelt's empathy for others, and Margaret Strecker's ethical understanding.

COMBINING YOUR ATTRIBUTES: AN UNSTOPPABLE SUPERPOWER

Consider all you have learned about physical, intellectual, social, emotional, and ethical development. Each area represents a different type of

Figure 10.1. Complexity

intelligence that you can master, with effort and commitment. These enhanced skills now surround you like a superpower. You can use them to understand and handle any problems that may come your way. They can be used discretely. However, as I said above, what makes them most effective is combining them to bring about successful emergence (see Figure 10.1).

For you Marvel fans, think of it like Thor's hammer, Captain America's shield, Iron Man's suit, Captain Marvel's strength, and Spiderman's reflexes. You can certainly achieve a lot with simply one superpower, but by combining your strengths simultaneously, you would be exceptional and unstoppable.

I can't possibly go over all the combinations of skills, but let's consider a handful to emphasize the point. For parents and teachers, imagine what your graduates would be like if they could master these skills as they enter the world beyond school—truly, a portrait of a graduate.

MASTERING SOCIAL AND EMOTIONAL INTELLIGENCE

This is Dr. Goleman's dream scenario. Combining social and emotional intelligence involves integrating and understanding one's own emotions and the emotions of others as well as the ability to navigate social interactions effectively. One will be able to use this awareness to network with people in a positive and empathetic manner.

For instance, a person will be able to recognize when they are feeling anxious in a social situation and understand how this might affect their interactions. They will be able to use strategies to manage their anxiety, such as deep breathing or positive self-talk, while also being mindful of how people around them are feeling.

In conversations, they listen actively to what others say, picking up on their verbal and nonverbal cues to understand their underlying emotions. They will respond with empathy, validating the other person's feelings.

In professional settings, they will excel at teamwork and building solid relationships. They will be relied on for their strong leadership skills and inspire and motivate others through authenticity and personal connection.

Have you ever been talking with a group at a social event when you noticed an acquaintance milling around looking for someone with whom to talk? In this situation, a person with emotional and social intelligence will be activated. They will be able to tell the other person is isolated and uncomfortable navigating the social dynamic. They will make eye contact and smile, inviting them over. When they arrive, they will open the circle so the other person can engage with the group. Know two things: one, they improved the other person's emotional disposition, and two, they improved the other person's ability to expand their own social skills.

MASTERING PHYSICAL AND INTELLECTUAL INTELLIGENCE

Combining physical and intellectual intelligence involves integrating bodily-kinesthetic and cognitive skills development. This integration allows one to connect one's mind and body and to leverage both domains to enhance one's intelligence and health.

Being proficient in physical and intellectual domains, a person will likely excel in activities like playing a musical instrument or participating in sports. When playing an instrument, one will be able to demonstrate technical skills, while fully understanding music theory. Similarly, in sports, one's physical prowess will allow one to combine strategic thinking, physical strength, and adaptability.

Can you remember when you last started playing a new sport? Imagine you are invited to play golf for the first time. You enjoy it. You go to the range, visit the putting green to practice, and even spend time chipping golf balls in the backyard. Physically, you get better, but you reach a plateau. While you are practicing, your friend mentions keeping your left arm straight. This little piece of intellectual advice helps your game; before you know it, you are researching several new techniques. You begin to master the game both physically and intellectually. You quickly realize the two intelligences enhance the effectiveness of each other.

MASTERING PHYSICAL, SOCIAL, AND ETHICAL INTELLIGENCE

Let's consider how this can be promoted in children. It is late on a Friday evening, and some friends are playing Ghost in the Graveyard. Two of them are running at full speed and collide, knocking each other down. An argument breaks out and emotions are running high given the violent nature of the outcome. Everyone starts to get involved in the dispute and the game is long forgotten. Someone has to think fast to save the evening—let's call her Debbie.

By combining physical, ethical, and social development, Debbie is well on her way toward Emergence.

Debbie has worked hard to become physically skilled, which has earned her the respect of her friends. She focuses on ethical and social development by promoting the importance of fair play. Ethical development involves nurturing character traits that guide her friends' behavior, and it intersects with physical and social development by encouraging honesty and compassion. Social development centers on acquiring interpersonal skills, which connect with physical and ethical development by fostering effective communication. Let's explore how this scenario could unfold.

Debbie respectfully calms everyone down and calls her friends over.

Debbie says, "Robin, were you trying to knock Christy down?" (Ethical)

She shakes her head and says, "I was running really fast and just tripped into her by accident." (Physical)

Debbie looks at Christy, "Aren't you good friends?" (Social)

She confirms, "Yes, but it hurt." (Physical)

Robin instinctively says, "I'm really sorry." (Ethical)

The game resumes.

Children can master these three attributes as a social group if raised with these skills. This is why it is important to promote all five intelligences simultaneously.

Mastering four developments and having a fifth underdeveloped attribute can produce the kind of individuals that are the pinnacle of destruction and chaos. Let's look at an example of this in the next section.

MASTERING INTELLECTUAL, SOCIAL, EMOTIONAL, AND PHYSICAL INTELLIGENCE: INCOMPETENT ETHICAL DEVELOPMENT

It might seem unusual, possibly even unethical, to use an example of a wicked individual when talking about mastering developments; however, if you give me a bit of leeway, I would like to use the most infamous individual in history to make a point about the importance of holistic self-development and the risks of ignoring just one attribute. Yes, let's examine Adolf Hitler.

He was a person with charismatic social skills, intellect, and emotional confidence, and he wielded physical intimidation along with completely corrupted ethical standards. Quite frankly, this combination is terrifying. He was able to think critically and creatively and manipulate those around him. He believed in himself and his ideals. He deftly used his social and emotional skills to convince entire groups of people to follow him, and he was physically capable of taking on a position of power that requires stamina.

However, his massive flaw, his unethical philosophies, and undeniably evil intentions proved to be a globally destructive force. The amount of devastation Hitler released upon Europe and Africa while convincing entire nations of people to participate in the Holocaust is unthinkable, yet it happened.

Under Hitler's command, six million Jews, along with millions of others considered undesirable by the regime, were systematically exterminated in concentration camps. The horrors of the Holocaust, with its gas chambers and systematic dehumanization, remain among the most egregious crimes in human history.

The war wrought havoc on civilian populations, leading to mass displacement and refugee crises of unprecedented proportions. Families were torn apart and forced to flee their homes in search of safety amid the carnage. Communities were shattered.

His propaganda and indoctrination sowed seeds of hatred and prejudice. Minorities were targeted while dissent was ruthlessly suppressed. The fabric of society frayed under the weight of hate, leaving scars that would linger long after Hitler's demise.

One man's twisted and unethical vision orchestrated unimaginable death, destruction, and hatred.

Hitler represents the worst kind of individual, and if not for a combination of allied countries, who knows what the world would look like today? Let's create another example.

MASTERING INTELLECTUAL, SOCIAL, EMOTIONAL, AND ETHICAL INTELLIGENCE: INCOMPETENT PHYSICAL DEVELOPMENT

Imagine being in a situation where you have worked your entire life to become wise, socially adept, emotionally stable, and ethically sound. However, you failed to consider the importance of physical health. I'm not talking about a little extra fold around your waistline, but living on fast foods and sugary sodas. Luckily, we have a real-world example to consider: a gentleman who experimented on himself using McDonald's.

Super Size Me is a documentary directed by Morgan Spurlock and released in 2004.[4] In the movie, Spurlock investigates the effects of exclusively consuming fast food from McDonald's for thirty days. He documents his experience and closely monitors his physical and mental health throughout. As Spurlock continues his fast-food diet, he experiences significant physical adverse effects. He gains weight rapidly, his cholesterol levels skyrocket, and he develops liver problems.

Additionally, he suffers from mood swings and lethargy and experiences a decrease in overall well-being. All this in just thirty days. What struck me about the documentary was how much impact one attribute (physical decline) can have on our other attributes if it's allowed to rapidly degrade, even if those other attributes were originally well developed. His mental well-being was severely impacted by being physically unhealthy, even though he was a happy person at the outset. His cognitive processes suffered. He felt less social. Even Kant would have said his behavior was unethical to himself.

Given my history, physical health is of particular importance to me. I think about it often. Stage IV cancer and cardiac arrest events both have low survival rates, and they cause continued difficulties in my life. Given this ever-present reminder, this is one of the reasons I emphatically mention how much you have to pay attention to your health.

Being forced to face death reminds me that our struggle to improve on this earth only lasts as long as we are here. You can always work to improve intellectually, socially, emotionally, and ethically. However, when your physical health reaches its nadir, the potential of all these other intelligences comes to an end. So, to maximize your time on earth and the length of your journey toward self-improvement, you need to commit to your health.

A HOLISTIC APPROACH TO DEVELOPMENT

As we've seen, poor physical health impacts your intellect, social skills, emotions, and ethics. We also know that poor ethics can result in warped emotions, negative influence, and distorted decision-making. It's clear that underdeveloped attributes result in deficiencies in other developmental areas.

For the longest time in education, we have seen and dealt with an individual's weakness in a siloed and compartmentalized way. Let's say a child is struggling with learning math in school. As a result, we communicate that with the parents: "Your child is struggling academically." In response, the teachers may give the child more practice, the parents may hire a tutor, and we might even take away the child's recess so they can finish their homework before they go home. Whatever the strategies employed, we tend to focus on the specific developmental area—intellectual problem in; intellectual solution out.

However, what would happen if we broadened our perspective when it comes to assessing the problem?

One astute teacher might recognize that, for instance, the child has no friends. He is isolated, sitting on a bench alone at recess, eating alone at lunch, and walking home alone daily. The teacher considers the child's life and speculates that the issue is social insecurity. They engage the counselor, and together, they help the child improve his social skills and build supportive connections in the school community. Within a short period, the child develops friendships, becomes happier, makes better decisions, and even runs around at recess. Finally, his grades improve. Intellect was never really the issue; rather, his social trauma was impeding all of his other attributes.

Indeed, while drafting my dissertation,[5] I came across studies highlighting "enhancers" that positively impacted intellectual development. In essence, if you improve your social skills, emotional well-being, ethical standards, and physical health, each area provides an intellectual boost.

Let's imagine those five developmental areas surrounding you again. However, this time, I want you to imagine that they are overlapping (see Figure 10.2).

Let's go back to our Marvel example. Imagine every time you were to upgrade Iron Man's suit, Thor's hammer got stronger, Captain Marvel's

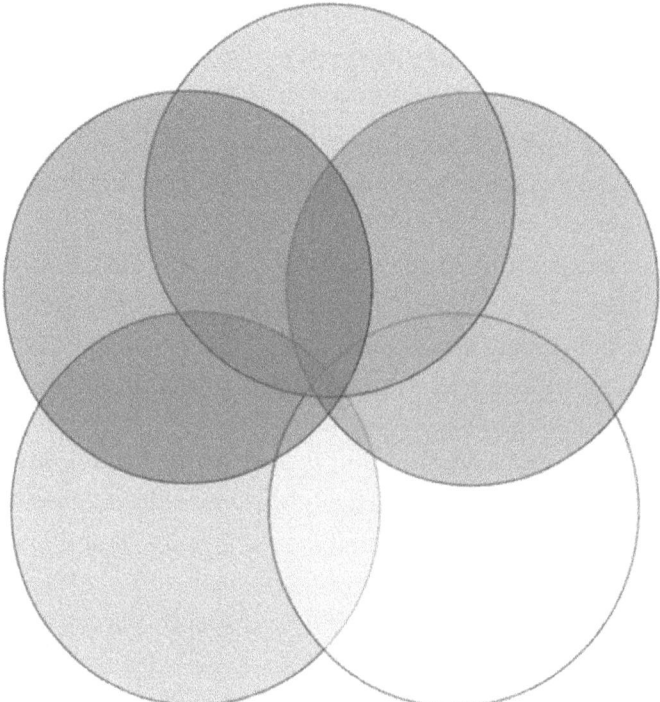

Figure 10.2. How the Five Attributes Overlap and Reinforce One Another

strength increased, Spider-Man became even faster, and Captain America's shield was more durable. That is what it is like to enhance your developmental skill building holistically. As you increase any of the five areas, the other four areas actually become more powerful.

Now imagine a person has developed all five intelligences simultaneously—they would become the superhero of superheroes. Let's create an example.

TRANSCENDENT EMERGENCE: MASTERING THE FIVE INTELLIGENCES

Having mastered all five areas of intelligence, no matter what a person's purpose or vision, they are now prepared to take on the complex task of bringing it to fruition.

For this exercise, I want you to imagine yourself being surrounded by your five areas of intelligence. Seriously, imagine it—floating orbs around you labeled as intellectual, social, emotional, ethical, and physical development. They all interconnect and self-reinforce. As you develop each, the orbs grow, indicating mastery.

As parents and teachers, we often acknowledge that the middle school years can be some of the most challenging for adolescents. During this time, they strive to become more intellectually capable, socially connected, emotionally confident, ethically responsible, and physically healthy. However, they often make mistakes along the way. Let me share one of the most difficult situations we may need to address.

Jessica is a very popular eighth grader. Her natural charisma is appealing, and drama seems to follow her wherever she goes. She is the envy of her friends, and the boys all like her. She is the most popular girl in school.

In this example, Jessica is both physically and socially intelligent. However, Jessica is struggling academically, emotionally, and ethically. She is struggling to keep up with her work, she feels she is not good enough, even though she would not share this with another soul, and she feels the way to maintain her popularity is to treat others in the class with disdain unless they are in her accepted group. I have experienced this situation countless times in my years in teaching, and it typically ends up in two ways.

1. Jessica continues down her current path, first isolating herself from those she mistreats. As they start to avoid her, she begins to treat her

friend group poorly as well. Ultimately, she becomes isolated with few to no friends. She minimizes the importance of academics as she seeks out further social cachet and struggles emotionally as things become more challenging. Her confidence continues to diminish, and she ultimately loses the qualities that once made her special. As a result, she loses her popularity, and the boys steer clear of her. To be honest, it is heartbreaking to watch as a parent or educator.
2. But there is another scenario, one based on the impact of Emergence. Jessica decides that her popularity is not nearly as important as her overall success. This might be due to a kind word from a teacher, a counselor, an administrator, or a parent. Truthfully, it could be anyone provided they are willing to invest time and energy. This is a tipping point for Jessica.
3. After a short stint of pressure from the members of her in-group, who love the drama she causes, they quickly grow to appreciate Jessica's newly developed kindness and support. She begins to receive social acceptance based on the positive attributes of integrity and empathy, not the chaos. As a result, her confidence grows. Her peers are willing to help her, and the faculty and staff appreciate her authentic efforts to improve herself academically. Intellectually, socially, emotionally, ethically, and physically she flourishes.

In the end, Jessica becomes the best version of herself. While true transcendence will take longer than her time through high school, a foundation has been laid to continue her journey toward Emergence. When this happens, if you were the person who helped Jessica, it is one of the most rewarding experiences in this world.

For Jessica, she is now intellectually, socially, emotionally, ethically, and physically gifted. Her world is open to endless possibilities. She has reached the rarified air of true Emergence.

As people, we often try to place people on this pedestal of exceptionality. Yet, most times we are disappointed. Try to think of a person who truly meets the criteria of all five intelligences. Even the people I have highlighted in the creation sections have their flaws.

Emergence is rare, but I hope through this book you have learned the pathway to reach it.

SUMMARY

- To develop a person's five attributes into true intelligence, they must apply Bloom's Taxonomy of Learning to each.
- Each area of intelligence reinforces the other four areas of intelligence.
- If one area is left to degrade—such as physical health—it can disrupt the entire system.
- To move from emergence to transcendence, a person must apply their five intelligences simultaneously.

PART III

ACHIEVING EMERGENCE: THE FIVE INTELLIGENCES

In Chapter 11, we will walk through the process of how to help your family and school make the emergence mindset a reality.

CHAPTER ELEVEN

BRINGING EMERGENCE TO FRUITION

Make your visions so clear, your fears become irrelevant.
—Anonymous

I want to use Chapter 11 as a map of how we can shift from the theoretical benefits of Emergence to practical application. Let's start with vision development.

In the center circle of Figure 11.1 is a single child. This could represent a son, a daughter, or a student in the classroom. Each child lives with you

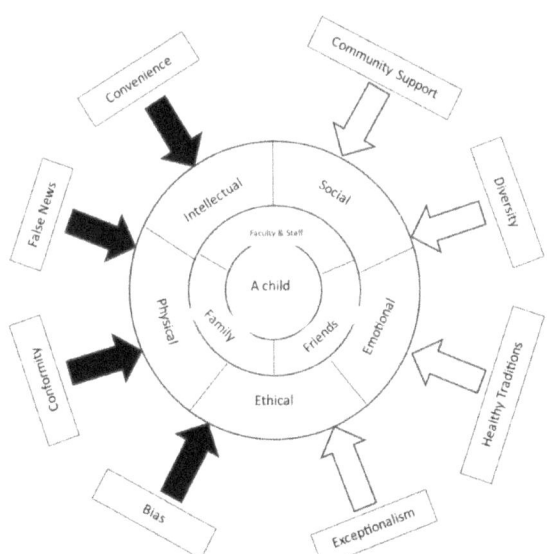

Figure 11.1. From the Perspective of a Child

and comes to school with their own initial conditions. They might be struggling to meet their physiological needs (food, clean water, and quality air to breathe), they might not have a home to live in or even experience the sensation of love and belonging. First things first; as families and schools, we need to try to meet these needs at all costs. Without these elements, it will be nearly impossible to self-actualize.

Also, we must consider their natural abilities—they might be of gifted intelligence or socially adept, or they might be physically disabled or emotionally fragile, or any combination in between. Regardless, we must work to meet the children where they are and progress them toward exceptionalism. This requires more than just testing for intellectual intelligence, so we must include the other four attributes, social, emotional, ethical, and physical intelligence, as part of the evaluation matrix.

- Does the child have any unmet physiological, safety, love and belonging, esteem, and actualization needs?
- What is the holistic baseline of abilities?

Next, the child is constantly taking in information from three critical groups—their families, their friends, and the faculty and staff at their schools (the second circle). Each group, in their own way, influences the child. This is why it proves difficult for a child to reach Emergence without strong, consistent role models such as friends, family, faculty, and staff. The child will certainly experience other impactful cultures you need to consider—churches, sports teams, etc. You should consider these cultures to determine whether they support or inhibit your child's maturation.

- Is your family consistently promoting intellectual growth, social skills, emotional regulation, ethical behaviors, and physical health?
- Are the teachers at your school promoting these attributes?
- Are your child's friends reinforcing these behaviors?

We have to realize that our responsibilities extend well beyond intellectual support. To help children reach their full potential, we must be willing to support them socially, emotionally, ethically, and physically as well (third circle). As families and schools, we must be consistent with cultivating a holistic culture based on these five intelligences. The third circle is about growth as laid out in Chapters 5–9. When we can foster an environment of all five elements of intelligence, using the six levels of Bloom's Taxonomy, we can facilitate Emergence.

As schools, we bear the responsibility of aligning the school, parents, and student culture to the core values. For schools, we must live and breathe these five intelligences every day. For parents, we must be willing to engage families in the process to understand the importance of the core values. For students, we must cultivate a culture of the core values. When all three elements are aligned, that is where an emergent culture is possible.

At Valley School, we host multiple opportunities for parents to be included in the process, including roller-skating nights, Idlewild gatherings, movie nights at school, state of the school addresses, parent conferences, concerts, musicals, athletic events, and I personally host grade-level parent groups at my home so the parents can create their own social groups. These opportunities are heavily attended.

We do the same with students, which includes most of the above and multiple rec nights, formal dances, school trips, clubs, hot chocolate days, and service opportunities. We even hosted a Halloween spectacular, behind the school in the woods. These make up a large part of the student's life.

If, and only if, we are able to come together as a collective of families, friends, faculty, and staff, will we be able to achieve our desired results.

In many ways, as I highlighted in Figure 11.1, our greater community also supports this endeavor. I have made note of the positive influences in Ligonier, Pennsylvania, represented with open arrows—community support, diversity, healthy traditions, and high expectations.

This helps buffer our community from the aspects of culture that foster discord.

I have highlighted these elements with closed arrows—overreaching convenience, fake news, conformity to bad choices, and biases. We understand the world will never be perfect, but this is why we need to help our students learn how to think, not just what to think. They need to discern wise advice from unhealthy influence.

So how do we accomplish this? Let's consider a vision development process that I have used to bring Emergent thinking to fruition.

BE SURE OF YOUR VISION

Let me share the story of a former student who initially made decisions without a vision.

"Maya" was a former student of mine who now lives in Chicago. She was always ambitious and chose to enter the field of medicine like her parents. I always thought medicine was her dream (her vision). I ran into her a decade later. Here is an account of our interaction.

After our initial excitement at seeing each other, she sounded unfulfilled when I asked her about her job. There was an emptiness in her. She told me she had achieved her desire to follow in her parents' footsteps, but she also told me she chose the profession only because her family had expected it. She was making a fine living but felt like she was missing something. She was considering a change.

After a nice fifteen-minute conversation, I told her to keep in touch. We exchanged contact information. When I caught up with her a few years later, she recounted what had happened after we last met.

One fall day, while walking along the beachfront near Navy Pier, she stumbled upon an old bookstore. Intrigued, she stepped inside. As she perused the bookshelves, her eyes landed on a dusty pile of used books. One book, in particular, caught her attention: *The 7 Habits of Highly Effective People* by Stephen Covey.[1] I know the book well.

Maya described flipping through the pages and discovering the second habit of the book—*the importance of beginning with the end in mind*. Covey highlights the importance of having a clear vision for one's life and making the most of each day. Struck by this insight, she embarked on a journey of self-discovery. She spent hours reflecting on her passions, dreams, and what truly mattered to her. Slowly but surely, a vision began to take shape in her mind—the idea of using her writing talents while remaining a doctor. She told me she poured her heart and soul into her work with newfound clarity. She started taking on service projects aligned with her values, using her writing to raise awareness for causes she believed in. Ultimately, she felt she had achieved the best of both worlds. She remained prosperous but, more importantly, she was happy and fulfilled.

To set goals without a clear vision can leave one unfulfilled even when we find financial stability. If we think back to Maslow's hierarchy, financial resources ensure safety and security, but they cannot provide love, esteem, or self-actualization. Maya had abundant security but was not fulfilled until she discovered and achieved her true vision.

So, using Covey's second habit, let's *begin with the end in mind*. Imagine your vision for your students or child in its most ideal circumstances. What does it look like? How would it feel to achieve it? Most importantly, how can you help your students and families define their own visions?

Please allow me to share my educational vision as an example: *To the best of my ability, I want to determine the most successful drivers of human development based on neuroscience, physics, biology, psychology, philosophy, and sociology and share them with the world. This starts in my own school—The Valley School of Ligonier.*

Now that we know what we want, do we have the passion to sustain it?

PASSION: THE DRIVING FORCE

> *You have to find something that you love enough to be able to take risks, jump over hurdles, and break through the brick walls that are always going to be placed in front of you.*
> —GEORGE LUCAS[2]

Passion is the essential, unrelenting force behind achieving your vision. I know daily life can wear away at your passions, especially for teachers and parents. This is why you must look for inspiration whenever you can. One of my childhood heroes, George Lucas, understood this idea intuitively. If done with intention and unrelenting will, it can change the world.

George Lucas was captivated by the magic of storytelling. He spent countless hours devouring books, immersing himself in their fictional, historic, future, and imaginary worlds. But the art of filmmaking was what truly ignited George's passion. He knew he had found his calling when he held a camera for the first time. With creativity and determination, George began experimenting with filmmaking.

Despite facing numerous challenges and setbacks along the way, George refused to give up on his dreams. He poured his heart and soul into his craft, honing his skills with each project he tackled. As he grew older, his talent caught the attention of others in the industry.

In 1973, George Lucas offered up his visionary masterpiece, *American Graffiti*.[3] The film was a critical and commercial success, earning George widespread acclaim and solidifying his status as a rising star in Hollywood. But George's greatest triumph was yet to come.

The year 1977 saw Lucas embark on an ambitious project: *Star Wars*.[4] Fueled by imagination and a relentless pursuit of perfection, George pushed the boundaries of filmmaking. Despite skepticism from studio executives, he persevered, pouring his heart and soul into every frame.

When *Star Wars* was finally released, it took the world by storm. Its groundbreaking special effects, compelling storytelling, and unique characters captivated audiences. The film became a cultural phenomenon, spawning an entire franchise that has thrilled audiences for generations.

But for George Lucas, *Star Wars* was more than "a movie"—it was the culmination of a lifelong passion, a testament to the power of dreams and the importance of never giving up on what you believe in. Through the realization of his dream, Lucas changed the face of cinema and inspired millions of people worldwide to believe in the power of imagination. Lucas's passion and pursuit of his vision led him down a path filled with adventure and wonder. His resulting achievement will be forever recalled as one of the greatest in the history of filmmaking.

As you can see, passion is for the creator, but the outcome is for the world. I remember my father taking me to see *Star Wars* in 1977. I thought it was the greatest thing I had ever seen. Even now, forty-eight years later, I can say that was my most impactful movie experience and that watching it with my father is one of my happiest memories. George Lucas's *Star Wars* universe deserves every accolade it has received. What a single person's passion can manifest in others is remarkable.

One of the reasons I take time to meet with every faculty member each year is to ensure they feel they are stoking their passions in the five areas of development. I know that if they maintain their passion for themselves and their work, they will do the same with the children in their care.

Are they intellectually stimulated, socially connected, emotionally well, ethically sound, and physically healthy? Has the administration cultivated an environment that promotes this level of human achievement in you? Are you doing this with your children or students?

Anything great that has ever intentionally happened is the result of tremendous passion. I can say unequivocally that the teachers at Valley are passionate in all five areas of development. This, in turn, inspires the children to be their best.

EXPERTISE: MASTERING THE LEARNING PROCESS

Now that you know how to help children define where they are going (vision) and help them develop the will to get there (passion), you need to support them in understanding a detailed learning process.

As you might have noticed from my earlier chapters, I used a distinct pattern of consideration for each of the five areas of intelligence. That pattern comes from Bloom.

Benjamin Bloom (1913–1999) was an American educational psychologist best known for his contributions to the field of education, particularly through the development of Bloom's Taxonomy.[5] Bloom's Taxonomy provides an effective breakdown of the human learning process, a tool we can rely upon to guide our journey toward true wisdom. Indeed, it's such a useful framework that I've used it to structure our learning in Part II of this book, in which we explore the five key intelligences of human development.

As you can see in Figure 11.2, knowledge (remembering) and comprehension (understanding) represent Levels 1 and 2 of Bloom's Taxonomy. In the mid-twentieth century, achieving these two levels of education may have been enough intelligence to make a career possible. However, the world has changed drastically since the taxonomy was first proposed.

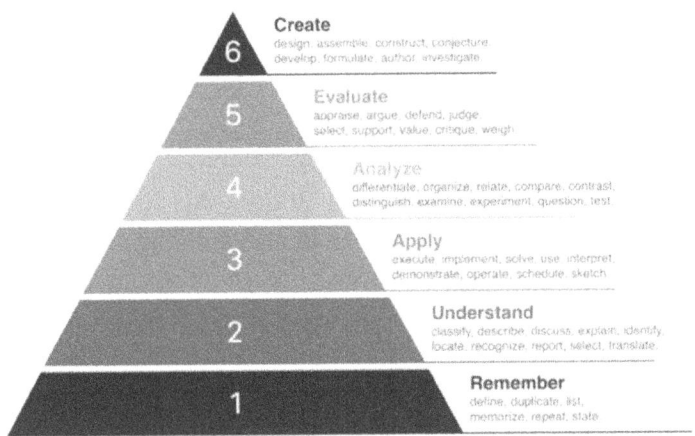

Figure 11.2. Bloom's Taxonomy (Revised 2001)

Indeed, it's changed considerably since it was revised in 2001, as well. One might claim the act of memorization and comprehension have been rendered almost useless with modern technology. You can look almost anything up on Google, YouTube, or ChatGPT. However, no matter how much information is available online, humans still need to have a certain amount of information embedded in their brains to support early learning processes.

Since I highlighted the importance of mathematics and English earlier, let me highlight the rest of the subject areas.

> **World Languages** play a crucial role in facilitating communication and fostering cultural understanding on a global scale, promoting international cooperation. Languages serve as bridges that connect people from diverse backgrounds. They enable the exchange of ideas and experiences across borders. By learning multiple languages, you gain access to a broader spectrum of perspectives and insights, enhancing your ability to navigate an increasingly interconnected world.
>
> **Science** serves as humanity's guiding light. It illuminates the mysteries of the universe and provides a systematic approach to understanding the world around us. Science empowers us to unravel the complexities of nature. Through observation, experimentation, and rigorous analysis, science drives innovation and fosters critical thinking skills essential for solving challenges. Science was crucial to the concepts we explored in Chapter 3, explaining the importance of complexity, including order and chaos.
>
> **History** is a vital repository of human experience, offering invaluable insights into the events that have shaped our world. By studying history, we gain a deeper understanding of human societies' triumphs and failures. It provides context for contemporary issues, helping us recognize patterns and make informed decisions. Additionally, history encourages civil conversations by fostering empathy and respect for differing perspectives. Through thoughtful examination of historical events and their consequences, you can engage in constructive dialogue and work toward common goals.
>
> **Performing and Visual Arts** education is indispensable in nurturing creativity, critical thinking, and cultural awareness. These subjects represent the highest levels of Bloom's Taxonomy. Through engagement with various forms of artistic expression, such as visual arts, music, theater, and dance, students develop the skills to communicate ideas and express

emotions. Beyond fostering artistic talent, arts education promotes innovation and problem-solving abilities. It prepares students for success in an increasingly complex and dynamic world. Without question, it enriches both society and individual lives.

Physical Education promotes overall health and well-being by encouraging regular physical activity and instilling lifelong fitness habits. It contributes to developing physical strength and endurance. Through playing team games, you learn essential skills around teamwork and sportsmanship, and these promote social integration and positive relationships. Most importantly, given our current lifestyles, physical education plays a crucial role in combating sedentary lifestyles and reducing the risk of chronic diseases such as obesity, diabetes, and cardiovascular disorders.

I could continue to list subject areas, including the importance of neurology, psychology, sociology, philosophy, and biology, which are all core elements of study we touched on in Chapters 5–9. Still, you get the point. These subjects are not as narrow in scope as their names might imply. They do not simply teach us about a range of information. They scaffold the essential building blocks of our brains' organization, rewiring us at a biological level to process information and develop our attitudes and behaviors. This is why when someone says they are "not a math person," I feel like telling them to think again. What they are really saying is that they can't successfully apply logic to situations, which, most of the time, is not true.

Let's briefly return to Bloom's Taxonomy to appreciate the depth of learning that is required to achieve expertise. People frequently say, "I want to learn more about _____." This is a positive step. However, what does it mean to learn compared to becoming wise about a particular topic? Bloom's Taxonomy—remembering, understanding, applying, analyzing, evaluating, and creating—is easy to understand but difficult to achieve. Let's consider the finer details together.

The first level is *remembering*. At this level, you can recall facts and basic concepts from memory. Think of the game show *Jeopardy!*[6] Remembering may involve recognizing and recalling information without necessarily understanding its meaning or context. It may seem simple, but remembering is foundational to higher-level cognitive processes. Essential memory allows your neurons to fire; other information can then attach to those active synapses. For example, think of an apple. What comes to mind?

- Apple—red or green, food, stem, worm, tree
- Apple—computer, iPad, iPhone, the Apple logo

However, the basic concept of an apple was embedded first, and then additional information was added. This additional information is contextualized, refined, and the concept advanced. For schools and parents, the practice of memorization, the precursor to *remembering*, has fallen out of favor. I encourage you to prioritize memory as an essential part of a six-stage learning process. Think of it as the foundation of a house, a base on which all other information is attached. With that said, if you are a teacher only embedding memory, children do not flourish with a concrete slab alone. They need scaffolding.

Moving up the hierarchy, the second level is *understanding*. At this level, a person can demonstrate comprehension by using their own words to interpret, explain, and summarize the information they have absorbed. Understanding goes beyond memorization and requires a person to grasp the meaning and significance of concepts. This level encourages a person to connect different pieces of information and relate new knowledge to their existing understanding.

Let's take a song lyric to make our point.

I'll never forget walking into a classroom where one of my students was repeating his initials, O.P.P. Without thinking, I started singing "O.P.P." by Naughty by Nature.[7]

The sixth graders all burst into laughter. They said, "Mr. Strecker (before I was Dr. Strecker), do you even know what that song is about?"

I said, "No clue."

They responded, "You need to listen to the lyrics."

I looked the lyrics up after class, and I turned as red as that apple I mentioned earlier.

I could recite the lyrics from memory. My brain pulled them up subconsciously. However, it wasn't until I actively considered the lyrics that I fully *understood* the song. Knowing what the lyrics are is remembering and knowing what they mean is understanding—a critical difference.

The third level of Bloom's Taxonomy is *application*. This is a person's ability to apply knowledge and concepts in new or unfamiliar situations.

This may involve performing tasks or making decisions based on acquired knowledge, transferring your understanding to real-world contexts.

Since my vision was to author a book, I had to spend a great deal of time refining my writing craft. I started my journey by authoring a sci-fi/horror novel called *Shimmers* in 2020, which is still available on Amazon.[8] I hoped the writing process would provide the necessary experience to begin *Emergence*.

If you are someone with an ambitious *vision*, consider taking on or suggesting a smaller initiative that will help you gain valuable application experience.

Moving further up the hierarchy, the fourth level is *analyzing*, my favorite part of learning. This is the ability to break down information into its constituent parts, identify patterns, and understand the relationship between elements. It involves examining information critically and dissecting it to discern underlying structures. This level encourages a person to think deeply about the content and explore its complexities and nuances.

For example, when I explored fractals in Chapter 1, I broke apart the process of complexity learning into manageable parts. These elements ultimately led to an epiphany. They are the building blocks of development, holistic success, self-reinforcement, and paradigm-shifting change.

The fifth level is *evaluation*. This is the ability to make judgments and assessments. Evaluation involves analyzing information critically and then going one step further to make recommendations as a person pursues their vision. In this way, a person develops their capacity for discernment and reflection holistically. Evaluating yourself and others equitably is a nuanced and complex process. Evaluation includes asking oneself the following questions when on a journey toward personal growth.

- Does our family or school have the intellectual expertise needed to accomplish their vision?
- Does our family or school have the emotional stability required to achieve their vision?
- Does our family or school have the social capacity to communicate their vision to others?
- Does our family or school have the ethical conviction to bring their vision to life equitably?
- Does our family or school have the physical stamina to reach their destination?

The sixth and final level of Bloom's Taxonomy is *creation*. Here, a person demonstrates their ability to integrate and combine information from different sources to build something entirely new. Synthesizing involves generating original ideas or solutions by reorganizing or restructuring existing knowledge. This level nurtures creativity and innovation.

Creation is the nexus point of a vision, a point of Emergence, where a person creates something unique and shares it with the world.

Visualize your brain as a network of roads. As you learn, progressing through Bloom's six levels, new roads are constructed. When connected, suddenly things that seem to be unrelated begin to link up, making sense of disparate concepts. As this complex web grows, the whole becomes more than the sum of its parts.

This process demonstrates the confluence of complexity theory and human development. For me, it was an epiphany. Every element in this book was, at one point, a discrete topic. The more I read, the more connections I made. These separate ideas eventually fit together into a framework of holistic understanding. That is the power of Bloom's sixth level of learning—creation.

Let's consider what this learning profile means for a school. Here are the things I considered as head of school:

Knowledge—What did I need to know?

- Elements of neurology, psychology, sociology, philosophy, and biology
- The definitions of concepts such as fractals, chaos, and order
- Maslow's Hierarchy
- Six Levels of Bloom's Taxonomy

Understanding—What did I need to comprehend?

- Why we are experiencing declines in our five core intelligences
- How complex thinking leads to Emergence
- The importance of finding a balance between order and chaos
- How my own past gave me insights into human development

Application—What did I need to apply?

- Cultivate an atmosphere of intellectual, social, emotional, ethical, and physical growth among the faculty, staff, parents, and students at Valley School.
- Ensure that we have the financial resources to accomplish this endeavor.

- Ensure that every facet of the school is centered on our vision, mission, and core values.

Analyze—What did I need to consider?

- Each department's needs—academic divisions, departments (athletic and art), support services, advancement, business office, safety and security, food services, facilities, etc.
- Constituent cultures—faculty, staff, parents, and students
- Community impressions

Evaluate—What did I need to appraise?

- The intellectual program (students)/professional development program (faculty and staff), and parent development (coffees/state of school)
- Social experiences—all constituency groups—maximizizing connections and collaboration
- Emotional health—all constituency groups—emotional regulation
- Ethical behaviors—all constituency groups—integrity
- Physical health—all constituency groups, including nutrition, sleep, and exercise

Create—What did I need to create?

- A school community that results in the Emergence of all constituency groups.
- A positive effect on other schools and greater society by writing a book.

GOALS: THE ROADMAP

You now understand the purpose of a vision and the importance of passion. You recognize what a person needs to learn and the depth of understanding required to become wise. Now is the time to develop goals—they will provide the roadmap to success.

Goals are indispensable tools in pursuing success as they provide a structured framework to transform a person's fleeting aspirations into tangible achievements. The SMART criteria—*specific, measurable, achievable, relevant,* and *time-bound* (Figure 11.3), first published by George Doran in 1981, offers a systematic approach to goal setting to enhance effectiveness.[9]

Figure 11.3. SMART Goals

To begin, goals must be *specific*, clearly defining what is to be accomplished, whether completing a project, achieving a particular grade, or mastering a skill. Specificity provides clarity and focus, guiding efforts toward a clear target with precision.

Secondly, goals should be *measurable*, allowing progress to be tracked and evaluated objectively. Measurable goals provide benchmarks against which a person can assess their advancement. Whether quantifiable in numbers, time, or milestones, they enable one to monitor their progress and make necessary adjustments.

We all have limited resources, time, and capabilities, so our goals must also be *achievable* and realistic. Sometimes, our passions can push us forward at an unattainable pace, and we bite off more than we can chew. While aspirations should stretch beyond one's comfort zone, setting unrealistic goals can lead to frustration. *Achievability* ensures that goals are within reach, enabling one to maintain momentum and sustain motivation and commitment.

Goals must be *relevant* and align with values, interests, and long-term objectives. Relevance ensures that goals are meaningful and worthwhile, inspiring one with an overarching purpose. When they resonate with aspirations and contribute to ambitions, a person is more likely to invest their time and energy wholeheartedly. Remember the Box System. Relevant goals should be aligned with core values.

Finally, goals should be *time-bound*, meaning they are anchored within a specific time limit for completion. Time-bound goals create a sense of urgency and accountability. They motivate one to take consistent action toward their realization. Setting deadlines and milestones enables one to maintain focus and avoid procrastination.

These criteria serve as essential guidelines for practical goal setting, ensuring that aspirations are translated into actionable plans with a higher likelihood of success. By crafting specific, measurable, achievable, relevant, and time-bound goals, you will navigate your journey successfully with clarity and purpose.

While the purpose of Emergence is to help our children, it is always wise to focus on yourself when developing skills. Take a moment to write down your SMART goals as a parent or teacher. Below each entry, I've written down my own SMART goals in regard to this endeavor, so you can see an example of how to approach this mental exercise.

Specific: _____

Example: I want to complete a book, *Emergence*, to help children achieve their dreams by creating a framework for personal development. This can be accomplished through families and schools using the concept of Emergence.

Measurable: _____

Example: I have hired editors (thank you, Art Fogartie, Sarah Busby, and Jessica Barbera) to hold me accountable for my writing progress. I can use the book to communicate this message to Valley School families, faculty, and staff.

Attainable: _____

Example: I've set aside time and funds for the writing process. I have practiced my writing craft by authoring another book, and I will use professional editors to help me complete the project.

Relevant: _____

Example: My overarching ambition is to support people who want to develop themselves. Regardless of the broader impact, however, at a minimum, it will be advice for my son and a personal accomplishment.

Time-Bound: _____

Example: I expect to finish writing in the spring of 2025 and have it published in spring 2026, after the editing and design process.

As a parent or teacher, you need to consider goals for your family and schools. Use the SMART method as a starting point.

POSITIVE MINDSET: THE FUEL

At this point, fatigue may begin to set in on this long journey. You must steel yourself for what comes next. Powerful results are fostered by a positive mindset.

A positive mindset serves as the cornerstone of personal growth and overall well-being. It is essential when driving the vision forward because it cultivates a focus on possibilities rather than limitations, which promotes optimism, perseverance, and adaptability when facing challenges. With a positive outlook, a person is more likely to approach obstacles as opportunities for growth. More generally, a positive mindset enhances mental health, strengthens relationships, and can foster a healthier lifestyle. It will empower one to navigate life's ups and downs with grace and gratitude. Ultimately, one will unlock their full potential and find their path to a more fulfilling and meaningful existence.

As we've discussed previously, the brain is adaptable. It connects neurons that fire simultaneously. If one maintains a positive mindset during complex and challenging times, one's brain will connect one's positive emotional center with any intellectual, social, ethical, or physical challenge.

But be careful: The opposite is also true. Let me provide a personal example.

When I was in middle school, I played basketball. Despite being one of the taller guys on the team, I rarely played more than a few minutes per game. In truth, I wasn't that great, and I knew it. I remember stepping onto the floor with an overwhelming sense of dread (fear neurons activated). But I stayed with it. I practiced relentlessly. By my junior year, I was the tallest member of the squad and I had improved my game. During the summer leagues, I played exceptionally well. The local paper put my picture on the front page. It was, by far, the pinnacle of my athletic career. However, this is not the feel-good story you might be anticipating.

When I ran onto the floor during our first varsity game, I was, on the face of it, perfectly prepared. I had done considerable physical work, developed my skills, and added another six inches to my frame. I received positive recognition from my coaches and teammates. But my brain, conditioned to be negative in that gym space, began imagining all the awful things that might happen during the game. I had not focused on changing my mental state. Because of that, I languished in mediocrity for the next two years and never reached my full potential. No matter how many practice shots I took or drills I ran, uncertainty, fear, and a negative mindset always emerged.

I have always felt bad about my inability to overcome those negative emotions. I never thought I was going to play professionally. But I know the terrific teams on which I played could have achieved so much more if I could have reached my own personal potential and contributed to their collective greatness.

I only understood the importance of a positive mindset after I went to college and began taking classes in neuropsychology. Once I came to see the brain as adaptable, I started forcing a positive attitude on myself, even during dire situations. The results were revolutionary.

So, let's consider how a person can begin to restructure their brain toward positivity. The brain fires continuously throughout the day. It adapts to the events we experience and the mindset we hold as things happen. This is why looking at events constructively fosters better thought patterns. Here are three things a person can do to foster a positive outlook, even when facing complex and difficult challenges, advice I picked up from Shawn Achor, author of *The Happiness Advantage*:[10]

1. Practice Gratitude—Whether during meditation, journaling, nightly prayers, or conversations with loved ones, be sure to thank yourself, God, or someone else for the positive people and things in your life. Your brain, influenced by this positive thought process, will begin to shape your life constructively.
2. Remain Mindful—It is important to maintain an awareness about *how* you're thinking. Your mindset is directly connected to your emotional center. However, it is your logic center that guides you to consider how you are choosing to process information. For many of us, when we respond negatively, there is a sense of being out of control. The way to take that control back is to process your responses in your logic center.

    The next time you get upset, go somewhere quiet and process that negative emotion. Imagine that negative emotion emanating from your response center, like a red-hot lightning bolt. Notice responses that tend to be reactionary. Now, visualize controlling and changing the

color from red to cool blue as you replace the negativity with positivity. That, my friend, is brain control. After some time, your brain will start to do this automatically.
3. Focus on Solutions—We have all faced challenges. As we experience difficulties, we tend to process them from problem-centric thinking or solution-oriented thinking. To ensure we remain positive rather than defeatist, we focus on solutions rather than the problem itself. Not only will you solve many more problems, but you will be seen as someone whom others can count on in times of need. That self-advocacy will begin to shape your brain for the better.

Imagine your perfect family and school in your mind's eye. Hold it there. Now begin looking for events that reinforce that belief, while minimizing events that work in direct contrast to that belief. Before you know it, you will be praising the people who deserve it, rather than constantly using energy on those who work against it.

DISCIPLINE: THE GUARDRAILS

Self-discipline is the cornerstone of personal growth and fulfillment. At its core, it is the ability to control impulses in pursuit of a vision. It empowers you to make conscious choices that align with your values rather than succumbing to the pull of instant gratification. By cultivating self-discipline, one develops strength in the face of obstacles, equipping you to overcome them.

I am sure you have faced setbacks in your own life. They may have been academic, financial, relational, or emotional. Whatever the disruptor, as you finish this book, you will now be able to help others develop the self-discipline required to overcome similar challenges.

Self-discipline fosters a sense of accountability for one's actions. Instead of relying on external factors to dictate a fate, a person takes ownership of their choices and their consequences. This sense of personal responsibility instills greater control within the chaos, empowering one to shape one's destiny.

There is a program for schools called *Responsibility-Centered Discipline* (*RCD*), otherwise known as responsive discipline. It promotes the *Give 'Em Five* Approach.

Excerpt from the Give 'Em Five website:

Support
—Use supportive statements that connect to your relationship with the student or identify a strength that she possesses.

Expectation
—Let the student know the expectations you have for him in the class.

Breakdown
—Communicate where you see the expectation breaking down or failing to be met.

Benefit
—Tell the student how meeting the expectation benefits her.

Closure
—Determine whether the situation has been resolved or whether the conversation is at a place where you can feel comfortable moving on.[11]

We all hit bumps in the road on our journeys toward our vision. I certainly did while writing this book. For a while, I stopped working on the book altogether. Here is how I handled it using the Give 'Em Five approach and positive self-talk:

1. Support—Jon, I know you really understand what this book could mean for people who wish to improve their lives. Even if you only help one person, it will be worth the effort.
2. Expectation—you promised yourself you would get this book done in 2025.
3. Breakdown—what you have been doing instead is filling your time with mindless entertainment.
4. Benefit—if you recommit yourself, your enthusiasm will be rekindled as it has multiple times before.
5. Closure—let's start by making a plan to reengage. Check for consistency.

Understanding these techniques for redirecting ourselves when we hit a wall in our progress forces us to become self-disciplined. This particular case involved effort, but it could be equally useful when the situation involves intellect, social skills, emotional response, and physical health.

RESILIENCE: THE ARMOR

As Frank Sinatra sang in "That's Life," some people get their kicks from "stomping on a dream."[12] A vision is difficult enough to bring to life without the scorn of others dragging it down. It requires all that we have discussed in this chapter and more. However, this final element—resilience—will drive one past the doubts, prove the naysayers wrong, and secure a person on the path to living their best life.

Resilience is imperative to one's well-being and success during adversity. A person will likely get knocked down again and again in the pursuit of their vision. If they accept defeat, no one can stop them from giving up. Resilience isn't just about struggling through setbacks; it's facing adversity head-on, learning from it, and emerging more robust and determined.

As you may have discerned, I am a movie buff. I love the messages hidden in films—what they teach us and how they make us feel. In a poignant moment from *Rocky Balboa* (2006), Rocky's son, Robert, blames his dad for the problems in his life. Robert feels he is always measured against his father. Robert worries that if Rocky proceeds with the fight, he will make a fool of himself and, by extension, his son. Rocky recognizes his son's lack of an independent spirit. Here is Rocky's response:

> Let me tell you something you already know. The world ain't all sunshine and rainbows. It's a very mean and nasty place, and I don't care how tough you are, it will beat you to your knees and keep you there permanently if you let it. You, me, or nobody is gonna hit as hard as life. But it ain't about how hard you get hit. It's about how hard you can get hit and keep moving forward. How much you can take and keep moving forward. That's how winning is done! Now if you know what you're worth then go out and get what you're worth. But ya gotta be willing to take the hits, and not pointing fingers saying you ain't where you wanna be because of him, or her, or anybody! Cowards do that and that ain't you! You're better than that![13]

This is just a movie clip, but watching it reminds me to be my best. (Don't tell anyone, but I get a little teary with inspiration.)

Figure 11.4 is the vision sequence. It is a visual reminder as to how to bring a vision to life.

Figure 11.4. Vision Sequence

I hope you have enjoyed our journey of Emergence. As I mentioned in Chapter 1, I know every great pyramid is built one fractal triangle at a time. I hope this book begins to allow you to create your foundation of stability and structure for your family or school.

ACKNOWLEDGMENTS

I want to thank my loving wife and son (Stacey and Josh), my mother (Margaret Strecker) and late father (Paul Strecker), my siblings (Angie, Heather, Matt, and Mark), dear friends whom I have mentioned throughout this book (Class of 1989—Bellevue High School), my schools (The Stanley Clark School, The John Cooper School, and Valley School of Ligonier), the faculty and staff I have had the pleasure to work with over the years, and, of course, all my students.

I would also like to thank my many mentors, including Mr. Michael Goodsite, Mr. Jim Tallman, Mr. Mike Maher, Dr. George Moore, Dr. Martinez-Garcia, Dr. Foster, Dr. Jones, Dr. Kiss, and my medical doctors, Dr. Thornton (who cured my stage IV cancer), Dr. Peoples (who brought me back after cardiac arrest), Dr. Lee, and Dr. Rihn (for keeping me alive).

Finally, thank you to my incredibly diligent editors—Art Fogartie, Sarah Busby, and Jessica Barbera.

Finally, *Emergence* is the culmination of many years of reading the work of intellectual titans. I have chosen to list some of my favorites below so you can begin your own journey into these subjects. After you have finished this book, regardless of the next volume you select, the information will fit nicely into your new emergent thinking framework.

Complexity—M. Mitchell Waldrop
Integrative Complexity Within Antitheses—Steve Carley
The 7 Habits of Highly Effective People and *The 8th Habit*—Stephen Covey
Simply Complexity—Neil Johnson
Primal Leadership, *Emotional Intelligence*, and *Social Intelligence*—Daniel Goleman
The Happiness Advantage and *Before Happiness*—Shawn Achor
Atomic Habits—James Clear
GRIT—Angela Duckworth

Good to Great—Jim Collins
The Four Agreements—Don Miguel Ruiz
The 5 AM Club—Robin Sharma
Disconnected—Thomas Kersting
Fierce Conversations—Susan Craig Scott
The Art of War—Sun Tzu
The Power of Positive Leadership—Jon Gordon
The Coddling of the American Mind—Jonathan Haidt and Greg Lukianoff
The Anxious Generation—Jonathan Haidt
Brainstorm and *The Yes Brain*—Daniel Siegel and Tina Payne Bryson
Start with Why—Simon Sinek
Balanced and Barefoot—Angela Hanscom
Mindset—Carol Dweck
Ethical Intelligence—Bruce Weinstein

There are many more, of course, but that's a good start.

NOTES

CHAPTER 1

1. *Schoolhouse Rock!*, episode 3, "Three Is a Magic Number," written by Bob Dorough, aired January 6, 1973, on ABC.
2. "Mission and Core Values," The Stanley Clark School, updated 2015, https://www.stanleyclark.org/about-us/mission-and-values.
3. "Mission, Philosophy, and Goals," The John Cooper School, updated 2019, https://www.johncooper.org/about/mission.
4. "About," Valley School of Ligonier, updated 2025, https://www.valleyschoolofligonier.org/about/welcome.
5. Nate Barksdale, "What Is Emergence?," John Templeton Foundation, February 15, 2023, https://www.templeton.org/news/what-is-emergence.

CHAPTER 2

1. Will Durant, *The Story of Philosophy: The Lives and Opinions of the World's Greatest Philosophers from Plato to John Dewey* (Pocket Books, 2006).
2. Olav Storsve, Jon Martin Sundet, Tore M. Torjussen, and Ole Christian Lang-Ree, "Flynn-effekten i Norge og andre land: Praktiske implikasjoner og teoretiske spørsmål" [The Flynn Effect in Norway and Other Countries: Practical Implications and Theoretical Questions], *Scandinavian Psychologist* 5 (2018): e6, https://psykologisk.no/sp/2018/08/e6/.
3. Tim Newcomb, "American IQ Scores Have Rapidly Dropped, Proving the 'Reverse Flynn Effect,'" *Popular Mechanics*, April 8, 2023, https://www.popularmechanics.com/science/a43469569/american-iq-scores-decline-reverse-flynn-effect/.
4. Nick deWilde, "The Social Architecture of Impactful Communities," Nick deWilde, August 20, 2020, https://www.nickdewilde.com/the-social-architecture-of-impactful-communities/.
5. "Opioid Epidemic, Poor State of Healthcare and Increased Time Spent Online Are Making Us MISERABLE as America Drops a Place on World Happiness Scale," *Daily Mail*, March 23, 2019, https://www.dailymail.co.uk/news/article-6843073/Americans-happy-theres-research-prove-it.html.
6. Kevin Vallier, "US Social Trust Has Fallen 23 Points Since 1964," *Kevin Vallier* (blog), November 30, 2020, https://www.kevinvallier.com/new-finding-us-social-trust-has-fallen-23-points-since-1964/.
7. Bernt Bratsberg and Ole Rogeberg, "Flynn Effect and Its Reversal Are Both Environmentally Caused," *Proceedings of the National Academy of Science* 115, no. 26 (2018): 6674–78, https://doi.org/10.1073/pnas.1718793115.
8. National Commission on Excellence in Education, *A Nation at Risk: The Imperative for Educational Reform* (NCEE, 1983).

9. No Child Left Behind Act, H.R. 1, 107th Cong. (2001).

10. Michele Salomon, "Mental Health: A Comprehensive Look at Harris Poll Research," Harris Poll, May 12, 2023, https://theharrispoll.com/briefs/mental-health-a-comprehensive-look-at-harris-poll-research.

11. Jonathan Haidt, *The Anxious Generation: How the Great Rewiring of Childhood Is Causing an Epidemic of Mental Illness* (Penguin, 2024).

12. Sara Lindberg, "Is Watching the News Bad for Your Mental Health?," Very Well Mind, May 21, 2024, https://www.verywellmind.com/is-watching-the-news-bad-for-mental-health-4802320.

13. "What About Me," MP3 audio, track 2 on Moving Pictures, *Days of Innocence*, Network / Wheatley, 1982.

CHAPTER 3

1. James Clear (@JamesClear), "Simplicity before understanding complexity is ignorance," Twitter (now X), April 13, 2020, https://x.com/JamesClear/status/1249814822977495046.

2. *A Beautiful Mind*, directed by Ron Howard (Universal Pictures, 2001), DVD.

3. M. Mitchell Waldrop, *Complexity: The Emerging Science at the Edge of Order and Chaos* (Simon & Schuster, 1992).

4. George Orwell, *1984* (Secker & Warburg, 1949; repr. Signet Classics, 2023).

5. Cormac McCarthy, *The Road* (Vintage International, 2006).

CHAPTER 4

1. *Jurassic Park*, directed by Steven Spielberg (Amblin Entertainment, 1993), DVD.

2. Tom Shatel, "The Unknown Barry Switzer—Poverty, Tragedy Build Oklahoma Coach into a Winner," *Chicago Tribune*, December 14, 1986, http://www.chicagotribune.com/news/ct-xpm-1986-12-14-8604030680-story.html.

3. Abraham H. Maslow, *A Theory of Human Motivation* (pub. by author, 1943; repr. Martino Fine Books, 2013).

4. "How Many Kids in the United States Live with Hunger?," No Kid Hungry, September 5, 2024, https://www.nokidhungry.org/blog/how-many-kids-united-states-live-hunger.

5. National Center for Education Statistics, *Student Bullying* (NCES, 2024).

CHAPTER 5

1. Mark Rippetoe, *Starting Strength: Basic Barbell Training*, 3rd ed. (Aasgaard Company, 2011).

2. "Obesity and Overweight," World Health Organization, March 1, 2024, https://www.who.int/news-room/fact-sheets/detail/obesity-and-overweight.

3. Sam Parker, *212° The Extra Degree: How to Achieve Results Beyond Your Wildest Expectations* (Walk the Talk, 2017).

4. Attributed to Jim Rohn (1930–2009), an American author and motivational speaker.

5. Ogie Shaw, "Winning the Mental Battle of Physical Fitness and Obesity," TEDx Talk, Spokane, WA, November 2014, 18 min., 31 sec., https://www.youtube.com/watch?v=K60xHx836T0.

6. Ibid.

7. Ibid.

8. *Tetris*, created by Alexey Pajitnov, 1985.

9. Attributed to Tony Horton (1958–present), an American personal trainer and author.

10. Tony Horton, *Bring It! The Revolutionary Fitness Plan for All Levels That Burns Fat, Builds Muscle, and Shreds Inches* (Rodale Books, 2012); Tony Horton, *The Big Picture: 11 Laws That Will Change Your Life* (Harper, 2014).

CHAPTER 6

1. Attributed to Albert Einstein (1879–1955), a German theoretical physicist and a pioneer in the field of quantum mechanics.
2. *WALL-E*, directed by Andrew Stanton (Walt Disney Studios, 2008), DVD.
3. Attributed to Socrates (d. 399 BCE), a Greek philosopher considered to be the father of Western philosophy and ethics.
4. "Uncle Tom's Cabin," MP3 audio, track 2 on Warrant, *Cherry Pie*, Columbia Records, 1990.
5. "The Marshmallow Test," video, posted April 21, 2010, by CBS, YouTube, https://www.youtube.com/watch?v=4y6R5boDqh4.
6. "Telegraph Line," *Schoolhouse Rock!*, last modified 2017, https://www.youtube.com/watch?v=ivk_irrH1WY.
7. Max Brooks, *World War Z: An Oral History of the Zombie War* (Broadway Books, 2006).
8. Albert Einstein, "Über einen die Erzeugung und Verwandlung des Lichtes betreffenden heuristischen Gesichtspunkt" [On a Heuristic Point of View About the Creation and Conversion of Light], *Annalen der Physik* 322, no. 6 (1905): 132–48; Albert Einstein, "Über die von der molekularkinetischen Theorie der Wärme geforderte Bewegung von in ruhenden Flüssigkeiten suspendierten Teilchen" [Investigations on the Theory of Brownian Movement], *Annalen der Physik* 322, no. 8 (1905): 549–60; Albert Einstein, "Zur Elektrodynamik bewegter Körper" [On the Electrodynamics of Moving Bodies], *Annalen der Physik* 322, no. 10 (1905): 891–921; Albert Einstein, "Ist die Trägheit eines Körpers von seinem Energieinhalt abhängig?" [Does the Inertia of a Body Depend upon Its Energy Content?], *Annalen der Physik* 323, no. 13 (1905): 639–41.
9. Albert Einstein, "The Field Equations of Gravitation," in *The Collected Papers of Albert Einstein*, ed. Robert Schulmann and Martin J. Klein, vol. 6, *The Berlin Years: Writings, 1914–1917* (Princeton University Press, 1996).

CHAPTER 7

1. Attributed to Mahatma Gandhi (1869–1948), an Indian anti-colonial nationalist and a pioneer in the use of nonviolent resistance in civil rights movements.
2. *Love on the Spectrum*, directed by Cian O'Clery, aired November 19, 2019–June 12, 2021, on ABC.
3. "I'm Yours," MP3 audio, track 2 on Jason Mraz, *We Sing. We Dance. We Steal Things*, Atlantic, 2008.
4. Daniel Goleman, *Social Intelligence: The Revolutionary New Science of Human Relationships* (Bantam, 2007).
5. Daniel Goleman, *Emotional Intelligence: Why It Can Matter More than IQ* (Bantam, 2005).
6. Daniel Goleman, Richard E. Boyatzis, and Annie McKee, *Primal Leadership: Unleashing the Power of Emotional Intelligence* (Harvard Business Review Press, 2013).
7. Goleman, *Social Intelligence*.
8. Giacomo Rizzolatti and Laila Craighero, "The Mirror-Neuron System," *Annual Review of Neuroscience* 27 (2004): 169–92.

9. George L. Kelling and James Q. Wilson, "Broken Windows," *Atlantic*, March 1982, https://www.theatlantic.com/magazine/archive/1982/03/broken-windows/304465.

10. Civil Rights Act of 1964, Pub. L. No. 88-352, 78 Stat. 241; Voting Rights Act of 1965, Pub. L. No. 89-110, 79 Stat. 437.

CHAPTER 8

1. Attributed to Guy Finley (b. 1949), a spiritual teacher and published self-help author.

2. "Social Media and Teen Mental Health," Annie E. Casey Foundation, August 10, 2023, https://www.aecf.org/blog/social-medias-concerning-effect-on-teen-mental-health.

3. Ibid.

4. Goleman, *Emotional Intelligence*.

5. *Merriam-Webster Dictionary*, "fear," last modified January 2, 2025, https://www.merriam-webster.com/dictionary/fear.

6. *Merriam-Webster Dictionary*, "anxiety," last modified December 22, 2024, https://www.merriam-webster.com/dictionary/anxiety.

7. *Rock Band*, created by Harmonix Music Systems, 2007.

8. Saul McLeod, "Pavlov's Dogs Experiment and Pavlovian Conditioning Response," *Simply Psychology*, February 2, 2024, https://www.simplypsychology.org/pavlov.html.

9. "First Lady of the World: Eleanor Roosevelt at Val-Kill," National Park Service, updated May 22, 2023, https://www.nps.gov/teachers/classrooms/26valkill.htm.

CHAPTER 9

1. Attributed to Immanuel Kant (1724–1804), a German philosopher and one of the leading figures in Western philosophy.

2. *Merriam-Webster Dictionary*, "ethics," last modified December 25, 2024, https://www.merriam-webster.com/dictionary/ethics.

3. Robert Johnson and Adam Cureton, "Kant's Moral Philosophy," in *Stanford Encyclopedia of Philosophy* (Stanford University, 1997–), published February 23, 2004; last modified October 2, 2025, https://plato.stanford.edu/entries/kant-moral.

4. Ibid.

5. Bruce Weinstein, *Ethical Intelligence: Five Principles for Untangling Your Toughest Problems at Work and Beyond* (New World Library, 2011).

6. *'Twas the Night Before Christmas*, written by Jerome Coopersmith, directed by Arthur Rankin Jr. and Jules Bass, aired December 8, 1974, on CBS.

7. Michael Barthel, Amy Mitchell, and Jesse Holcomb, "Many Americans Believe Fake News Is Sowing Confusion," Pew Research Center, December 15, 2016, https://www.pewresearch.org/journalism/2016/12/15/many-americans-believe-fake-news-is-sowing-confusion.

8. Jeffrey M. Jones, "Most Americans Would Believe Social Media Misinformation Warnings," Knight Foundation, October 13, 2020, https://knightfoundation.org/articles/most-americans-would-believe-social-media-misinformation-warnings.

9. Steve Alder, "Healthcare Data Breach Statistics," *HIPAA Journal*, December 30, 2024, https://www.hipaajournal.com/healthcare-data-breach-statistics.

10. "FTC Staff Reminds Influencers and Brands to Clearly Disclose Relationship," Federal Trade Commission, April 19, 2017, https://www.ftc.gov/news-events/news/press-releases/2017/04/ftc-staff-reminds-influencers-brands-clearly-disclose-relationship.

11. Matthew Tyler, Justin Grimmer, and Shanto Iyengar, "Partisan Enclaves and Information Bazaars: Mapping Selective Exposure to Online News," *Journal of Politics* 84, no. 2 (2022): 1057–73.

12. "Instagram Ranked Worst for Young People's Mental Health," Royal Society for Public Health, May 19, 2017, https://www.rsph.org.uk/about-us/news/instagram-ranked-worst-for-young-people-s-mental-health.html.

13. J. W. Patchin and S. Hinduja, "Cyberbullying Facts," Cyberbullying Research Center, 2024, https://cyberbullying.org/facts.

14. *Star Trek II: The Wrath of Khan*, directed by Nicholas Meyer (Paramount Pictures, 1982), DVD.

CHAPTER 10

1. Attributed to Aristotle (384–322 BCE), a Greek philosopher and inventor of formal logic.

2. *Merriam-Webster Dictionary*, "complex," last modified December 25, 2024, https://www.merriam-webster.com/dictionary/complex.

3. Timothy B. Jones, "Complexity Theory," in *The Handbook of Educational Theories*, ed. Beverly J. Irby (Information Age Publishing, Inc., 2013); Fritjof Capra, *The Turning Point: Science, Society, and the Rising Culture* (Bantam, 1984); Fritjof Capra, *The Web of Life: A New Scientific Understanding of Living Systems* (Anchor, 1997); *Mindwalk*, directed by Bernt Capra (Triton Pictures, 1990), DVD.

4. *Super Size Me*, directed by Morgan Spurlock (The Con, 2004), DVD.

5. J. P. Strecker, "Private Middle School Principal Perceptions and Experiences Regarding Educational Culture and Student Development (Protocol No. 2015-11-26968)." Doctoral diss., Sam Houston State University, 2016.

CHAPTER 11

1. Stephen R. Covey, *The 7 Habits of Highly Effective People: Powerful Lessons in Personal Change* (Free Press, 2004).

2. Attributed to George Lucas (b. 1944), an American filmmaker and philanthropist known for creating the *Star Wars* and *Indiana Jones* franchises.

3. *American Graffiti*, directed by George Lucas (Lucasfilm, 1973), DVD.

4. *Star Wars*, directed by George Lucas (Lucasfilm, 1977–present), DVD.

5. Benjamin S. Bloom, *The Taxonomy of Educational Objectives: The Classification of Educational Goals* (David McKay Company, 1956).

6. *Jeopardy!*, created by Merv Griffin, aired March 30, 1964–present.

7. "O.P.P.," MP3 audio, track 3 on Naughty by Nature, *Naughty by Nature*, Tommy Boy Records, 1991.

8. J. P. Strecker, *Shimmers* (pub. by author, 2020).

9. George T. Doran, "There's a S.M.A.R.T. Way to Write Management's Goals and Objectives," *Management Review* 70, no. 11 (1981): 35–36.

10. Shawn Achor, *The Happiness Advantage: The Seven Principles of Positive Psychology That Fuel Success and Performance at Work* (Crown Business, 2010).

11. "Responsibility-Centered Discipline," Give 'Em Five, accessed January 5, 2025, https://www.givemfive.com.

12. "That's Life," MP3 audio, track 1 on Frank Sinatra, *That's Life*, Reprise Records, 1966.

13. *Rocky Balboa*, directed by Sylvester Stallone (Metro-Goldwyn-Mayer, 2006), DVD.

BIBLIOGRAPHY

Achor, Shawn. *The Happiness Advantage: The Seven Principles of Positive Psychology That Fuel Success and Performance at Work*. Crown Business, 2010.

Alder, Steve. "Healthcare Data Breach Statistics." *HIPAA Journal*, December 30, 2024. https://www.hipaajournal.com/healthcare-data-breach-statistics.

Annie E. Casey Foundation. "Social Media and Teen Mental Health." August 10, 2023. https://www.aecf.org/blog/social-medias-concerning-effect-on-teen-mental-health.

Barksdale, Nate. "What Is Emergence?" John Templeton Foundation, February 15, 2023. https://www.templeton.org/news/what-is-emergence.

Barthel, Michael, Amy Mitchell, and Jesse Holcomb. "Many Americans Believe Fake News Is Sowing Confusion." Pew Research Center, December 15, 2016. https://www.pewresearch.org/journalism/2016/12/15/many-americans-believe-fake-news-is-sowing-confusion.

Bloom, Benjamin S. *The Taxonomy of Educational Objectives: The Classification of Educational Goals*. David McKay Company, 1956.

Bratsberg, Bernt, and Ole Rogeberg. "Flynn Effect and Its Reversal Are Both Environmentally Caused." *Proceedings of the National Academy of Science* 115, no. 26 (2018): 6674–78. https://doi.org/10.1073/pnas.1718793115.

Brooks, Max. *World War Z: An Oral History of the Zombie War*. Broadway Books, 2006.

Capra, Bernt, director. *Mindwalk*. Triton Pictures, 1990.

Capra, Fritjof. *The Turning Point: Science, Society, and the Rising Culture*. Bantam, 1984.

———. *The Web of Life: A New Scientific Understanding of Living Systems*. Anchor, 1997.

Covey, Stephen R. *The 7 Habits of Highly Effective People: Powerful Lessons in Personal Change*. Free Press, 2004.

deWilde, Nick. "The Social Architecture of Impactful Communities." Nick deWilde, August 20, 2020. https://www.nickdewilde.com/the-social-architecture-of-impactful-communities/.

Doran, George T. "There's a S.M.A.R.T. Way to Write Management's Goals and Objectives." *Management Review* 70, no. 11 (1981): 35–36.

Durant, Will. *The Story of Philosophy: The Lives and Opinions of the World's Greatest Philosophers from Plato to John Dewey*. Pocket Books, 2006.

Einstein, Albert. "Ist die Trägheit eines Körpers von seinem Energieinhalt abhängig?" [Does the Inertia of a Body Depend upon Its Energy Content?]. *Annalen der Physik* 323, no. 13 (1905): 639–41.

———. "The Field Equations of Gravitation." In *The Berlin Years: Writings, 1914–1917*, vol. 6 of *The Collected Papers of Albert Einstein*, edited by Robert Schulmann and Martin J. Klein. Princeton University Press, 1996.

———. "Zur Elektrodynamik bewegter Körper" [On the Electrodynamics of Moving Bodies]. *Annalen der Physik* 322, no. 10 (1905): 891–921.

———. "Über die von der molekularkinetischen Theorie der Wärme geforderte Bewegung von in ruhenden Flüssigkeiten suspendierten Teilchen" [Investigations on the Theory of Brownian Movement]. *Annalen der Physik* 322, no. 8 (1905): 549–60.

———. "Über einen die Erzeugung und Verwandlung des Lichtes betreffenden heuristischen Gesichtspunkt" [On a Heuristic Point of View About the Creation and Conversion of Light]. *Annalen der Physik* 322, no. 6 (1905): 132–48.

Federal Trade Commission. "FTC Staff Reminds Influencers and Brands to Clearly Disclose Relationship." April 19, 2017. https://www.ftc.gov/news-events/news/press-releases/2017/04/ftc-staff-reminds-influencers-brands-clearly-disclose-relationship.

Give 'Em Five. "Responsibility-Centered Discipline." Accessed January 5, 2025. https://www.givemfive.com.

Goleman, Daniel. *Emotional Intelligence: Why It Can Matter More than IQ*. Bantam, 2005.

———. *Social Intelligence: The Revolutionary New Science of Human Relationships*. Bantam, 2007.

Goleman, Daniel, Richard E. Boyatzis, and Annie McKee. *Primal Leadership: Unleashing the Power of Emotional Intelligence*. Harvard Business Review Press, 2013.

Griffin, Merv, creator. *Jeopardy!* Aired March 30, 1964–present, on NBC.

Haidt, Jonathan. *The Anxious Generation: How the Great Rewiring of Childhood Is Causing an Epidemic of Mental Illness*. Penguin, 2024.

Horton, Tony. *Bring It! The Revolutionary Fitness Plan for All Levels That Burns Fat, Builds Muscle, and Shreds Inches*. Rodale Books, 2012.

———. *The Big Picture: 11 Laws That Will Change Your Life*. Harper, 2014.

Howard, Ron, director. *A Beautiful Mind*. Universal Pictures, 2001.

Johnson, Robert, and Adam Cureton. "Kant's Moral Philosophy." In *Stanford Encyclopedia of Philosophy*. Stanford University, 1997–. Article published February 23, 2004; last modified October 2, 2025. https://plato.stanford.edu/entries/kant-moral.

John Cooper School, The. "Mission, Philosophy, and Goals." Updated 2019. https://www.johncooper.org/about/mission.

John Templeton Foundation. "Vision, Mission & Impact." Accessed November 1, 2024. https://www.templeton.org/about/vision-mission-impact.

Jones, Jeffrey M. "Most Americans Would Believe Social Media Misinformation Warnings." Knight Foundation, October 13, 2020. https://knightfoundation.org/articles/most-americans-would-believe-social-media-misinformation-warnings/.

Jones, Neil D. *Computability and Complexity: From a Programming Perspective*. MIT Press, 1997.

Jones, T. B. "Complexity Theory," in *The Handbook of Educational Theories*, edited by Beverly J. Irby. Information Age Publishing, Inc., 2013.

Kelling, George L., and James Q. Wilson. "Broken Windows." *Atlantic*, March 1982. https://www.theatlantic.com/magazine/archive/1982/03/broken-windows/304465.

Lindberg, Sara. "Is Watching the News Bad for Your Mental Health?" Very Well Mind, May 21, 2024. https://www.verywellmind.com/is-watching-the-news-bad-for-mental-health-4802320.

Lucas, George, director. *American Graffiti*. Lucasfilm, 1973.

———. *Star Wars*. Lucasfilm, 1977–present.

"Marshmallow Test, The." Video. April 21, 2010. CBS, YouTube, 2 min., 43 sec. https://www.youtube.com/watch?v=4y6R5boDqh4.

Maslow, Abraham H. *A Theory of Human Motivation*. Martino Fine Books, 2013. Originally published by the author, 1943.

McCarthy, Cormac. *The Road*. Vintage International, 2006.

McLeod, Saul. "Pavlov's Dogs Experiment and Pavlovian Conditioning Response." *Simply Psychology*, February 2, 2024. https://www.simplypsychology.org/pavlov.html.

Meyer, Nicholas, director. *Star Trek II: The Wrath of Khan*. Paramount Pictures, 1982.

Moving Pictures. *Days of Innocence*. Produced by Charles Fisher. Network (US); Wheatley (Australia). Released January 1982.

Mraz, Jason. *We Sing. We Dance. We Steal Things.* Produced by Martin Terefe. Atlantic. Released May 12, 2008.

National Center for Education Statistics. *Student Bullying*. NCES, 2024.

National Commission on Excellence in Education. *A Nation at Risk: The Imperative for Educational Reform*. NCEE, 1983.

National Park Service. "First Lady of the World: Eleanor Roosevelt at Val-Kill." Updated May 22, 2023. https://www.nps.gov/teachers/classrooms/26valkill.htm.

Naughty by Nature. *Naughty by Nature*. Produced by Naughty by Nature. Tommy Boy Records. Released September 3, 1991.

Newcomb, Tim. "American IQ Scores Have Rapidly Dropped, Proving the 'Reverse Flynn Effect.'" *Popular Mechanics*, April 8, 2023. https://www.popularmechanics.com/science/a43469569/american-iq-scores-decline-reverse-flynn-effect/.

No Kid Hungry. "How Many Kids in the United States Live with Hunger?" September 5, 2024. https://www.nokidhungry.org/blog/how-many-kids-united-states-live-hunger.

O'Clery, Cian, director. *Love on the Spectrum*. Aired November 19, 2019–June 12, 2021, on ABC.

"Opioid Epidemic, Poor State of Healthcare and Increased Time Spent Online Are Making Us MISERABLE as America Drops a Place on World Happiness Scale." *Daily Mail*, March 23, 2019. https://www.dailymail.co.uk/news/article-6843073/Americans-happy-theres-research-prove-it.html.

Orwell, George. *1984*. Signet Classics, 2023. Originally published in 1949 by Secker & Warburg.

Parker, Sam. *212° The Extra Degree: How to Achieve Results Beyond Your Wildest Expectations*. Walk the Talk, 2017.

Patchin, J. W., and S. Hinduja. "Cyberbullying Facts." Cyberbullying Research Center, 2024. https://cyberbullying.org/facts.

Rankin, Arthur, Jr., and Jules Bass, directors. *'Twas the Night Before Christmas*. Written by Jerome Coopersmith. Aired December 8, 1974, on CBS.

Rippetoe, Mark. *Starting Strength: Basic Barbell Training*. 3rd ed. Aasgaard Company, 2011.

Rizzolatti, Giacomo, and Laila Craighero. "The Mirror-Neuron System." *Annual Review of Neuroscience* 27 (2004): 169–92.

Royal Society for Public Health. "Instagram Ranked Worst for Young People's Mental Health." May 19, 2017. https://www.rsph.org.uk/about-us/news/instagram-ranked-worst-for-young-people-s-mental-health.html.

Salomon, Michele. "Mental Health: A Comprehensive Look at Harris Poll Research." Harris Poll, May 12, 2023. https://theharrispoll.com/briefs/mental-health-a-comprehensive-look-at-harris-poll-research.

Schoolhouse Rock! "Telegraph Line." https://www.youtube.com/watch?v=ivk_irrH1WY.

Schoolhouse Rock! Episode 3, "Three Is a Magic Number." Aired January 6, 1973, on ABC.

Shatel, Tom. "The Unknown Barry Switzer—Poverty, Tragedy Build Oklahoma Coach into a Winner." *Chicago Tribune*, December 14, 1986. http://www.chicagotribune.com/news/ct-xpm-1986-12-14-8604030680-story.html.

Shaw, Ogie. "Winning the Mental Battle of Physical Fitness and Obesity." TEDx Talk, Spokane, WA, November 2014. 18 min., 31 sec. https://www.youtube.com/watch?v=K60xHx836T0.

Sinatra, Frank. *That's Life*. Produced by Jimmy Bowen. Reprise Records. Released November 18, 1966.

Spielberg, Steven, director. *Jurassic Park*. Amblin Entertainment, 1993.

Spurlock, Morgan, director. *Super Size Me*. The Con, 2004.

Stallone, Sylvester, director. *Rocky Balboa*. Metro-Goldwyn-Mayer, 2006.

Stanley Clark School, The. "Mission and Core Values." Updated 2015. https://www.stanleyclark.org/about-us/mission-and-values.

Stanton, Andrew, director. *WALL-E*. Walt Disney Studios, 2008.

Storsve, Olav, Jon Martin Sundet, Tore M. Torjussen, and Ole Christian Lang-Ree. "Flynn-effekten i Norge og andre land: Praktiske implikasjoner og teoretiske spørsmål" [The Flynn Effect in Norway and Other Countries: Practical Implications and Theoretical Questions]. *Scandinavian Psychologist* 5 (2018): e6. https://psykologisk.no/sp/2018/08/e6/.

Strecker, J. P. "Private Middle School Principal Perceptions and Experiences Regarding Educational Culture and Student Development (Protocol No. 2015-11-26968)." Doctoral diss., Sam Houston State University, 2016.

Strecker, J. P. *Shimmers*. Published by the author, 2020.

Tyler, Matthew, Justin Grimmer, and Shanto Iyengar. "Partisan Enclaves and Information Bazaars: Mapping Selective Exposure to Online News." *Journal of Politics* 84, no. 2 (2022): 1057–73.

Valley School of Ligonier. "About." Updated 2025. https://www.valleyschoolofligonier.org/about/welcome.

Vallier, Kevin. "US Social Trust Has Fallen 23 Points Since 1964." *Kevin Vallier* (blog), November 30, 2020. https://www.kevinvallier.com/new-finding-us-social-trust-has-fallen-23-points-since-1964/.

Waldrop, M. Mitchell. *Complexity: The Emerging Science at the Edge of Order and Chaos*. Simon & Schuster, 1992.

Warrant. *Cherry Pie*. Produced by Beau Hill. Columbia Records. Released September 11, 1990.

Weinstein, Bruce. *Ethical Intelligence: Five Principles for Untangling Your Toughest Problems at Work and Beyond*. New World Library, 2011.

World Health Organization. "Obesity and Overweight." March 1, 2024. https://www.who.int/news-room/fact-sheets/detail/obesity-and-overweight.

www.ingramcontent.com/pod-product-compliance
Ingram Content Group UK Ltd.
Pitfield, Milton Keynes, MK11 3LW, UK
UKHW041822310326
5020IPUK00002B/21